# The Art of Argument

## A Guide to Mooting

CHRISTOPHER KEE

CAMBRIDGE UNIVERSITY PRESS
Cambridge, New York, Melbourne, Madrid, Cape Town,
Singapore, São Paulo, Delhi, Tokyo, Mexico City

Cambridge University Press
The Edinburgh Building, Cambridge CB2 8RU, UK

Published in the United States of America by
Cambridge University Press, New York

www.cambridge.org
Information on this title: www.cambridge.org/9780521685139

First published 2006

*A catalogue record for this publication is available from the British Library*

*Library of Congress Cataloguing in Publication data*
Christopher Kee
The Art of Argument: A Guide to Mooting
Bibliography.
Includes index.
ISBN-13 978-0-52168-513-9 paperback
ISBN-10 0-52168-513-3 paperback
1. Debates and debating – Handbooks, manuals, etc.    I. Title.
808.53

ISBN 978-0-521-68513-9 Paperback

# The Art of Argument
## A Guide to Mooting

There is no greater skill for a law student than constructing a logical and compelling argument. *The Art of Argument: A Guide to Mooting* guides the reader through the process of developing, presenting and defending a convincing argument in an international mooting competition – a setting where students from around the world come together to argue a hypothetical case and hone their skills as advocates.

The book explains the secrets of success in mooting, in a simple, step-by-step style. It describes:

- what to do when you first get the moot problem
- how to begin researching the subject matter
- how to build an argument
- how to present written and oral submissions
- the value of practice moots
- how to handle yourself at the competition.

This book is primarily aimed at students who are preparing to participate in an international mooting competition. However, other students will find the techniques applicable in all areas of their study and exam preparation, and coaches of moot teams will find it an invaluable source of hints, tips and useful advice.

**Christopher Kee** is a lecturer in law at Deakin University, with a private practice in the field of arbitration. He has an extraordinary record of success as a participant and coach in domestic and international moot teams.

# Contents

**Part 3:  International moots**

# Preface

Every book has a purpose and this one is no different. This book is primarily aimed at students who are interested in participating in an international mooting competition. However, many of the strategies outlined in the book apply also to domestic moots, as well as to general preparation for exams and assignments. Many coaches of moot teams will find the tips suggested in this book to be extremely helpful in achieving success for their team.

The book is based on the fundamental premise that mooting, and in particular mooting at international competitions, should be fun. The fact that you are participating in a competition is simply the framework that will enable you to have fun. Winning the competition should not be your ultimate goal. Winning is certainly a worthy goal and achievement. However, the knowledge and experience you acquire along the way, and the lifelong friends you will make, are ultimately worth more than your name on a trophy.

In 1999 I was part of the Deakin University team that participated in and won the oral hearings of the Willem C Vis International Arbitration Moot held in Vienna, Austria. I have also coached teams to success in other moot competitions. At the inaugural Madhav Rao Scindia International Moot Court Competition, hosted by the University of Delhi, my students won three of the four prizes on offer, including winning the moot itself. In addition, my students have won numerous individual awards. So when you read this book be assured that it is written from experience. I understand intimately the process you are about to embark upon. I have been through the emotional highs and lows, and I know how to win.

This book is written in a style that is designed to speak to you. It is both informal and informative. It is not a stuffy legal text that spouts rules of law that you must obey. On the contrary, this book encourages you to be creative, and to think about issues in new ways. It is a "how to" book that concentrates on practical aspects of mooting to assist you through the process; its focus is not the law that may sometimes weigh heavily on your shoulders.

I want to share my secrets of success because I do not believe they should be secrets. Mooting is a very worthwhile educative tool. Through the process of mooting you learn how to construct analytical arguments, to present your point logically and soundly, and to consider and address the queries and concerns of your opponent and the moot master. For a law student there is no greater skill than constructing a logical and compelling argument. High-level international moot competitions are probably the closest you will get to a real legal case, while you are still a student. By this I mean a case that you are responsible for: a case where you are the advocate, and where your client's future depends on your ability to argue.

International moots serve an even greater purpose. By their very nature, international moot competitions are examples of disputes that are solved in a peaceful and non-violent manner. At a time in history we may come to remember for its acts of horrific violence and its "war on terror", it is comforting to know that some disputes can still be resolved amicably and reasonably. With all this in mind, I wish you good luck as you embark upon your journey. I know that you will find this book useful, and I ask that you never forget the most important piece of advice I can give you – have fun!

# Acknowledgments

There are many people who deserve recognition and thanks, because without their assistance this book would not have been written: Jill Henry at Cambridge University Press, who patiently guided me through this process; Catherine Ng, who provided nearly all the references and annotations relating to intellectual property; Professor Eric Bergsten, Louise Barrington and Michael Peil, who are directors of the Vis Moot, Vis Moot (East) and Jessup Moot respectively; my moot teams, who perhaps without realising it, identified many of the areas I have written on; and my colleagues at Keelins and Deakin who manage to put up with me. Particular thanks must be given to my parents, Kevin and Patricia Kee, and my brother Michael Kee. My family has been a great source of support and inspiration, not to mention proofreaders. The last thank you is the most important. Professor Jeff Waincymer was my coach when I participated in the Vis Moot. It was he who taught me the secrets of success. I attribute many of the things I have achieved in my professional career to my participation in the moot. I will be forever grateful for all that he taught me.

Christopher Kee
Lecturer, School of Law, Deakin University

Part 1

# Making the most of a moot

# Chapter 1

# Introduction

## WHAT IS MOOTING?

*The adjective* moot *is originally a legal term going back to the mid-16th century. It derives from the noun* moot, *in its sense of a hypothetical case argued as an exercise by law students. Consequently, a moot question is one that is arguable or open to debate. But in the mid-19th century people also began to look at the hypothetical side of moot as its essential meaning, and they started to use the word to mean "of no significance or relevance". Thus, a moot point, however debatable, is one that has no practical value. . . . When using* moot *one should be sure that the context makes clear which sense is meant.*

The American Heritage® Dictionary of the English Language, Fourth Edition, Copyright © 2000 by Houghton Mifflin Company

The way in which the word *moot* is used has evolved over time, as the introductory quote indicates. However, for our purposes we need to stick with the original mid 16th century meaning. When you participate in an international mooting competition, you will be part of a group of law students engaging in the exercise of arguing a hypothetical case. This definition remains true whether you are presented with an extremely detailed set of facts or a very brief two-page problem; whether you are arguing your case before an arbitral tribunal or before a court of law. In any case, there are two very important aspects of law you will need to be familiar with: the law governing the substance of the case, usually simply called the substantive law; and the law governing the procedure used to determine the dispute, usually called the procedural law.

# WHY JOIN A MOOT TEAM?

There are so many reasons why someone might want to be part of a moot team that it is difficult to limit the list. Here are five important reasons.

## Job opportunities

Participation in an international mooting competition can increase your job opportunities in a variety of ways. The section of the book called "Make the most of your opportunities" explains them in much more detail (see pages 106–7).

Experience in international mooting is a very impressive addition to your resume. Although there are increasing numbers of students participating in mooting competitions, it will remain a fairly exclusive club for many years to come, and will give you an edge over others applying for the same job. For all the reasons we will discuss in this book, your participation will not only make you a better candidate, but will also better prepare you to go about the task of actually getting the job, for example, by helping you perform well in interviews.

International mooting competitions are great networking opportunities. If you are an impressive candidate you will always do well, but having good contacts will be an added bonus. You will meet new friends and new business contacts – often the very people you have just spent six months reading about.

## Team work

Until now, whenever you have worked in a team as a student, you have probably had a say in who the team members were. In many cases your team members will have been your friends. It is fun to work with your friends, but when you are practising in the field of law you are more likely to find yourself in a team of people you do not know well, some of whom you may even dislike.

You need to learn how to work as part of a team that you did not choose. Often participation in an international mooting team will be the first time you experience this situation. It is not always easy, but it will prepare you well for your working career. Employers value this kind of experience. They are looking for people who know how to function in a team.

## Intensive training

When you go to a moot competition you are representing your university, your country and most importantly yourself. For those reasons alone you will want to perform well. To perform well you will need to undergo intensive training. How much training you do is up to you. Some teams will do several practice moots a week for weeks on end to improve their skills. Others will have spent hours and hours ensconced in a library researching particular points of law and learning the subject matter backwards. You will gain knowledge and valuable skills by the time you complete this process, and the intensive training you undertake along the way will help you to deal with many other aspects of your life beyond the law.

## International travel

Although the various international moot competitions are structured in different ways, all of them have the prospect of international travel. For those more fortunate students whose universities are well funded, it is likely that this travel will be heavily subsidised. But even if your university is not in a position to assist you, a moot competition gives you a very compelling excuse to catch that travel bug and go overseas. Having made the investment to travel to a moot, many students take advantage of their location and have a holiday following the end of competition. This can be one of the best experiences of your life.

For many of you it may be your first venture outside the country, and the experience will be life-changing. You may not appreciate it when you first meet your team, but you will be grateful to be travelling with people you know.

## New perspectives

In many ways this reason is the product of all the reasons listed. You will be introduced to many new experiences through your involvement in an international moot. Each new experience will force you to challenge your existing perspectives, an invaluable lesson that will serve you well as you enter the legal profession.

# HOW TO USE THIS BOOK

This book is designed to be used in a variety of ways. Start by reading Part 1 from beginning to end. This should not take a lot of time. Then you can refer back to the book as the need arises. Each chapter deals either with a discrete point in the process of the competition, or a general issue that could arise at any time. For example, when you are practising your presentations, you might want to refer to the presentation tips and look over the strategies for working in a team when someone is really annoying you. A consequence of this structure is that the chapter lengths vary considerably. While each topic is important, chapters 4, 5, 6 and 7 contain what might be described as the substantive aspects of the book.

Now you know why you should want to be part of a moot team and how to use this book. Good luck in making the team!

# Chapter 2

# You've made the team – what next?

## BEFORE YOU BEGIN

Good preparation is the key to success in mooting competitions. This book aims to give you an insight into issues you are likely to encounter throughout the process. This means that you can begin preparing for all aspects now, rather than have problems descend on you at a time when your efforts are better spent refining your oral presentations.

## Timing and commitment

We have already noted that participation in a moot competition involves intensive training. With intensive training comes commitment. A team will set its own level of commitment, but if you want your team to perform at its best, every member needs to be highly committed to ensure the team's success.

Participating in an international mooting competition involves an extraordinary amount of time. It takes time to prepare. It takes time to travel overseas and participate. All of this needs planning. In particular, you need to think about what impact it will have on other commitments you may have, such as paid employment, other studies, and family relationships. Paid employment is potentially the most difficult to accommodate.

The time of year when the moot actually takes place needs careful consideration when you are deciding whether or not to participate. For example, a moot that takes place in the early part of the year will require most students in the southern hemisphere to work solidly throughout their summer break. There are advantages and disadvantages to this. First, you will not need to divert your attention from other subjects that also demand and deserve your attention. However, equally, you will not be able to pursue recreational activities and relaxation during your holiday time. Days spent at the beach are likely to be replaced by days spent in the library. Perhaps more significantly, the full-time work you had hoped to do over summer may not be possible.

A moot held during the year may conflict with important academic events such as exams and due dates for assignments. If this occurs you will need to consult your tutors and lecturers to see if alternative arrangements can be made.

# What about money?

For some fortunate students, money will not be an issue, but for many it is a very big concern. Unfortunately, participating in an international mooting competition does cost money, whether that is simply the entrance fee, or includes the costs of flights and accommodation while you are overseas.

Think about where the money is going to come from at this early stage. You do not want to find yourself distracted by this issue while you are trying to devote all your attention to preparing and practising your arguments.

Because the situation for every team is different, it is important that all members sit down together and discuss this issue. There are several options you could consider and you need to work out what will best suit your team.

### Everyone pays for themselves

The most obvious option is that everyone pays for themselves. However, this can be riddled with difficulties. Not everyone in your team is likely to have the same capacity to fund their trip. Since you are participating as a team, you should travel together and stay in the same accommodation to really make it a team experience. But some people simply will not be able to afford to stay in some hotels or to travel on particular airlines. This can lead to difficult decisions that need to be made as a team. It also means that financial status becomes a discriminating factor. There will be those who simply cannot compete if they are required to fund their own participation.

This is a great shame, as every student could benefit greatly from this experience.

## Sponsorship

The alternative (or in addition) to everyone personally contributing is for your team to obtain sponsorship. Sponsorship can come from a range of sources. Your law school is the most obvious potential source. Depending on how your particular educational institution is structured you may be able to get sponsorship from different parts of the university as well. Other potential sources of funding are law firms and private benefactors. The advantage of sponsorship is that it creates a pool of money that every member of the team can benefit from equally.

As a team you may choose to nominate someone or a couple of people who, in return for some lighter research duties, spend some time on raising sponsorship. There are definite advantages in directing your sponsorship efforts in this way. Primarily it ensures that you have a coordinated approach. Potential sponsors will get frustrated if five different people from the same team individually approach them to ask for sponsorship. It is also more efficient for team members to focus on particular areas, rather than every member attempting to spend some time on all the team tasks. Some team members can concentrate on detailed research while others can focus on raising money.

If your team decides to nominate one or two people to seek sponsorship, it is very important that you choose the right people within your group to take on the task. Within any team there will be mix of personalities. It is important that you recognise that each of you has different strengths. In order to learn to operate well as a team, you need to work out how to fully utilise everyone's individual strengths. Fundraising generally requires a very outgoing personality. You will only be successful if you willingly take on the task, bearing in mind that it is a big job. Some of the challenges involved may only become apparent once you begin. For example, you may need to coordinate your fundraising efforts with those of other groups within your law school that are also seeking sponsorship, such as other moot teams and the law students' society.

The task of fundraising carries with it significant responsibility, and therefore can place real pressure on the relationships in the team. As a team you should ensure that you set realistic fundraising targets. It is much better to underestimate what you think you can raise. If for whatever reason your team ultimately fails to reach the intended target, make sure you pause and think of the best interests of the team before you rush to blame your designated fundraiser.

# THE MOOT PROBLEM

## Read the problem

There is a great deal of excitement when you first receive the moot problem. Everyone is different and approaches the first reading their own way. Some people read every word of every line very carefully; others just glance over it and think the answers are obvious! As you would expect, these people are in for a surprise and will very quickly learn that first impressions rarely reflect final ones.

The best approach is probably somewhere in the middle. Sit down and read the problem carefully. There is no need to be too meticulous the first time you look at it; instead you want to absorb the basic information and facts, so you can begin to plan how you might tackle the problem. Read it over once, maybe twice if you want to, and then put it aside and just think about it for a day or so. Sleep on it!

Many students, when reading their moot problem for the first time, think, "I have absolutely no idea what this is about!" By their very nature, international moot competitions deal with complex international legal questions, and therefore the subject matter tends to be outside the ordinary curriculum. Do not be alarmed by the subject matter. All it means is that you are about to face a very steep learning curve. Over the next few weeks you are going to absorb lots and lots of new information. Far from being a bad thing, this is a wonderful challenge that should excite you.

## Read the rules of the competition

A crucial task is to familiarise yourself with the rules of the competition. Each competition will have its own set of rules, and you need to know exactly how the rules affect how you should prepare, before you begin to solve the moot problem. Imagine you had done months and months of research and handed in your written submissions, and were then told that you would have won an award but unfortunately you had used the wrong citation method. Or you attended the oral hearings and got perfect scores for all of them, but because you only argued the applicant's case in each moot, you were not eligible for the best oralist award.

The rules of the competition will influence the way you prepare, so it is very important that you are familiar with them right from the beginning. For example, there may be rules about how you can use the evidence provided in the moot problem. It would be a waste of valuable time to practise using the evidence in a different way.

Be aware that the rules of a particular competition may conflict with some of the recommendations in this book. This book is written as generally as possible and aims to develop themes that are consistent with most if not all advocacy, whether in international or domestic moots, or in professional practice. However, there may be occasions where particular rules prohibit the use of some of the techniques discussed. In particular, you should be aware of the extent to which the rules of the competition allow you to utilise external assistance. If the rules do conflict with a technique outlined here, think about the purpose of the technique suggested and find a way to achieve the same outcome within the rules.

## ASKING FOR HELP

You need to find a quick way of gaining a rudimentary understanding of the subject matter. Once you have the basics then you can develop your ideas and start to come to grips with the complexities of the issues. It would be a good idea to do a "crash course" in the area. Usually this is something that your coach will coordinate for you. But you can be proactive and take steps as a team to begin the learning process.

There are many people you can turn to for help. Your coach will be your first port of call, and within your law school there will be lecturers with specialities in all sorts of disciplines, who will be a great resource for you.

If your law school has been participating in a moot competition for some years, you should seek out former participants. Arguably there are no better people to give you an understanding of what will be required. Consulting former moot participants can be a vital part of achieving success, an approach we return to later in the book (see pages 96–7).

Other students at your law school may also be able to help. Part of your subject matter might be taught briefly in an optional unit taken late in your degree. If so, find students who have taken that subject and ask them to speak to the team. Ask the lecturers if there are any post-graduate students who have an interest in the subject matter. Post-graduate students can be a great resource as they are usually experienced researchers who can offer many tips.

You might also consider approaching law firms, particularly those you already have a relationship with, such as the ones who may be sponsoring your team. Generally people will be willing to offer their assistance if they know that you appreciate and value their effort. On this note, it is very important to thank everyone who gives up their time to help you.

# SETTING DEADLINES

The task of estimating the time required to complete a project is often one of the hardest. In one of the *Star Trek* movies, Captain Kirk asks Scotty how he always manages to get things done ahead of the estimated time. Scotty's reply was that he estimated how long it would take and then tripled it before telling the Captain when to expect the work to be completed. This is a very sensible idea.

Break down the process of preparing for the moot into individual tasks, and estimate how long each will take. This is a difficult job and your coach will help you. Start by asking yourself when the first task is due. Do you have a matter of weeks or months? Only rarely do things go to plan, so make sure you have enough time to accommodate any unexpected obstacles. Be careful though not to fall into the trap of thinking the deadlines you set are always flexible. Once you set a deadline always work to it.

# Chapter 3

# Being part of a team

## THE KEYS TO A SUCCESSFUL TEAM

### Attitude

The attitude you as an individual bring to working in the team will affect both the way the team functions and the value of your experience. You must have a positive attitude about every member in your team. It is often said that the secret of a successful marriage is to work on it every day; the same is true of a successful team.

Although we leave the analysis of human behaviour to other disciplines such as psychology and psychiatry, lawyers are keen observers. An immediate observation we can make is that no two people are the same. We will all have had different experiences in life, which will lead us to think differently and deal with problems in different ways. Working as part of a team requires you to respect the differences that exist between team members. It can be a difficult and challenging task, particularly when you are teamed with someone you find very annoying. However, it is a skill that will hold you in very good stead throughout your professional career.

There is no doubt that your attitude towards your team-mates will be tested often. Someone will do something (or probably more often not do something) that is a cause of great frustration and annoyance to you. It is during those times that you have to work the hardest on the team relationship.

## Identify strengths and weaknesses in the team

The best way to maintain a positive attitude towards everyone in your team is to identify and focus on their respective strengths. It stands to reason that different people will have different strengths and weaknesses. If as a team you are able to work together and complement each member's strengths, collectively you will make a formidable combination.

The process of identifying and discussing the strengths and weaknesses within the team can be a personally challenging one. It will force you to be very honest with yourself about your own abilities. Sometimes it will be relatively easy to see what each team member brings, particularly where the team members have been specifically chosen by a coach. On other occasions it may not be so easy. In all teams, no matter how they have been composed, every team member brings something positive and beneficial to the team. It is very important that you remember this throughout the entire period of the moot.

In general there are three sorts of occasions where the recognition of strengths is particularly necessary. The first is during your initial team meeting when you are deciding how to allocate tasks. The second two occasions are more personal: when you begin to question your own involvement, and when you are frustrated by your colleagues.

## Dealing with a crisis of confidence

It is almost inevitable that during any intense and demanding task you will begin to question your own value and abilities. During these times it is very easy for your judgment to become clouded by what you perceive (probably incorrectly) as overwhelming weaknesses. For example, if you are struggling to understand a particular point that the rest of the team appeared to comprehend instantaneously you might begin to feel intellectually inadequate. Alternatively, after a series of less than perfect moot performances, you may decide that you will never make a good advocate.

In these situations, your attitude is key. Just because you are not the intellectual genius of the team, or you may not be as good an advocate as some of the others, does not mean that your contribution to the team is any less important. If the other members of your team cannot explain a particular point to you, then they need to work on how to explain it better. Remember that advocacy is about presenting a convincing argument. If the argument cannot be understood, it most certainly cannot be genuinely convincing. The perfect argument will be one that is understood by everyone. The exercise your team-mates go through, helping you to understand the point, will serve everyone well for when the argument is presented in a moot. It will identify how the argument should be built, and what aspects must be conveyed so that everyone can appreciate the point.

If you do find yourself in the middle of a minor crisis of this kind, do not get overwhelmed by it. Focus on the positives that you do bring to the team. Do something that you have no doubt you are really good at. In time your confidence will return. It is just a matter of patience and practice.

Remember that contributions to the team are not limited to adding to arguments or mooting well. Helping the team to function effectively as a team can at times have a greater impact on success or failure. You might be particularly good at understanding the particular dynamic of your team. If so then you may be able to quietly and subtly work on certain team-mates to avoid a confrontation between them. Alternatively, you may be able to provide a little extra support to a team member who is suffering from a temporary bout of self-doubt. Yet another possibility is that you may use your natural assertiveness to ensure that those who are less assertive are still heard by the rest of the team. There really is no end to the types of positive contributions that you can make.

## Maintaining trust

A team is built on trust. Any time you believe a team member has let you or the team down, a little bit of trust is lost. Focusing on the positive attributes of team members helps restore that trust, and conversely forgetting their positives can widen the rift.

During periods of tension within the team, and there are likely to be many, it is important to think carefully before you speak. Rash words said in anger or frustration can cause considerable damage. Accusations that someone has let the team down are rarely, if ever, going to be beneficial to the team as a whole.

Think about your objective. In a team environment this should always be for the team to function as effectively as it can to achieve the team goals. Think about the person you are talking to. How will the person react to what you are going to say? Do not assume that because you would not be hurt by a sarcastic comment, your team-mate would not be hurt. Remember you are different people.

Consideration of your audience is a very important part of advocacy. It applies equally to moot masters as it does to team-mates. Indeed you will probably find that as you progress through the preparation of your case, the general manner in which you argue within the team (and in your life generally) will begin to change.

## Do you need to be friends?

How people come to be part of a moot team will vary enormously. Sometimes it will be a group of friends who have heard of the moot and convince their law school to participate. On other occasions the law school will have an established mooting program. In this situation it is quite possible that you will not know everyone in the team before you begin working together. Alternatively, you may know your team members, but not like some of them. In any of these situations, your feelings towards your team-mates are likely to change over the period of the moot. Friendships can be made and existing relationships may sour. The key to dealing with these trials and tribulations is to remain professional.

The experience of the team-work involved in international moot competitions is one that will hold you in good stead when you join the profession, and will make you more attractive to potential employers. In the typical group activities at university, it is very easy to avoid developing your team-work skills. Students will often choose the group they work in, and inevitably choose their friends. The lack of time and intensity required by these standard tasks mean that there is very little stress placed on friendships within a group. In other cases, if students have been allocated to a group, tasks are often divided in such a way that people are effectively working individually rather than as a team. For example, the group may be required to complete a series of small tasks and each member completes one task. This may be an equitable distribution of the workload but it defeats the purpose of the team activity.

A moot problem that requires attention over a sustained period of time does not allow you to avoid team issues. It operates in much the same way as if you were working on a problem in a law firm. Very few people have the luxury of working with friends at first. Over time we may become friendly with our work colleagues, but at the beginning they are an unknown quantity, just as we are to them. One of the questions potential employers often ask about applicants is how this person will fit into our workplace. You will be able to draw upon your moot competition experience to demonstrate you are familiar with working in a team. You will probably also be able to say that during the process you managed to make very good friendships with your team-mates.

# Chapter 4

# Building an argument

This is one of the most important chapters of this book. The principles outlined here apply not only in the context of the mooting competition, but equally in legal practice. As an advocate in a moot or in professional practice you need to develop and deliver a compelling and convincing argument to support your case.

So how do you build an argument? There are a variety of approaches you might take. The method suggested below is only one option. However, a feature of most successful approaches is a defined structure.

## THE BASIC STEPS

Before you start to build an argument, think about how you are going to develop the structure of your argument, and most importantly think about how you are going to test it.

## Step 1 – Read the facts and decide instinctively who should win

Whenever you encounter a set of facts, you will instinctively form an opinion of who should win. This is human nature. Your opinion will be influenced by many factors, from the way the problem is presented to the personal experiences that have shaped your beliefs and values. For example, we each have our own notions of what is fair and just, and of what is right and wrong. These are emotive and subjective responses. For most people, their emotive and subjective responses will be the instinctive ones. As an advocate you will need to either exploit or overcome these emotive and subjective responses, depending on which side you are representing.

Your own instinctive response will be influenced by your training. A legal education trains you to have a response that goes beyond subjective prejudice. Lawyers are taught to think objectively. We do our best to remove emotion from a conflict and to apply the law "without fear or favour". Legal philosophers may debate whether ultimately this is a good or bad thing, but as a general rule it is what judges and arbitrators are called upon to do.

Once you have identified instinctively who should win, influenced by your legal knowledge and training, you have the base from which you can build your arguments. Bear in mind that well-written moot problems will tend not to be designed so that one side is clearly favoured, so irrespective of who you are representing, there will be prejudices that work for and against your arguments.

## Step 2 – Identify who you are representing

At first this may seem a little obvious. Naturally you need to identify which party you are acting for! But the question goes deeper than that. You need to remember that you are representing the client's case – not yours. Make sure that you stay sufficiently objective so that you can identify weaknesses in your own case. This is reasonably easy to do in a moot case, but it can be much more difficult in real cases when you are dealing with a flesh-and-blood client whose future may depend on the outcome.

Over the time you spend building your arguments you will have made a considerable emotional investment in your case. You will feel some ownership of your arguments and may tend to become protective of them. While it is very important to be willing to defend all your arguments, it must be a "defence" and not simply a dismissal of the criticism.

In moot competitions this issue tends to display itself within the team, particularly if any of the team members are battling insecurities. One member of the team will come up with an argument that they think is compelling, and another member of the team will disagree – and the battle ensues. This process should be seen to be constructive rather than obstructive. Ideally every argument by every team member should be criticised, as criticism will either confirm the validity of the argument or lead to its improvement.

## Step 3 – Compile a list of arguments

Now that you are confident and comfortable that you are representing a party and not simply your own pet arguments, begin compiling a list of reasons why your side should win. These need to be reasoned and supported arguments. The untrained and instinctive responses we talked about above are examples of unreasoned and unsupported arguments, which need to be developed. For example, "just because it is right" is not a reasoned argument. You need to explain why it is right.

You need to immerse yourself in research. This is when you begin to learn the complexities of the subject matter. Your arguments must be supported by primary sources, such as the law itself, and secondary sources, such as commentaries. What amounts to a primary or secondary source will depend on the area of law you are dealing with.

You should be very careful to avoid false reasoning. In simple examples, it can be easy to identify an error of logic in an argument. For example: all dogs have four legs; this cat has four legs; this cat is a dog. However, when the propositions in an argument are much more complex, it can be difficult to spot problems with the reasoning.

It is very important to write or record your arguments as you develop them. During later stages of the process, you will need to be able to review every stage of the argument's development.

In a nutshell, then, your task is to prepare the longest list of reasoned and supported arguments you possibly can to persuade any moot master that your client should win. Structure the list so that your most convincing points are at the top and the really weak arguments are at the bottom. Set yourself a time limit to complete this task, bearing in mind the overall time pressures that you face.

## Step 4 – Imagine you represent the other side

This step is harder than step 3 as it involves more work. You now have two tasks. You need to develop a response to every one of the arguments in the list you have prepared, thus simultaneously develop an equally reasoned and supported list of arguments why the opposing side should now win.

Why do we do this? Some advocates argue that the way to build the strongest case for your client is to first build the case for the other side. In doing so you effectively identify the weaknesses in your case and the challenges you will need to meet. Being aware of all the weak points in your case allows you to build stronger arguments.

Sometimes criticising your earlier arguments can be an easy task, if you have already come across authorities that support an opposing view during your initial research. If you made a note of these authorities, you can now go back to them and use them to support your new arguments. On other occasions it will not be as easy, and the process will take some time. Make sure that at every stage you are recording the development of each of your arguments.

# Step 5 – Repeat steps 3 and 4 at least five times

At first, you might think that repeating steps 3 and 4 at least five times seems tedious and unnecessary. But do not take an ordinary approach to answering your moot problem. Most people will work on an argument until they reach the first obvious "clear win" for one side. However, to use a card game analogy, there are never any trumps in mooting. If you believe you have arrived at the perfect argument for your client, you do so at your own peril. It is dangerous simply because you have stopped developing the argument. What happens when, while sitting in the final of a moot competition, your opponent delivers an effective response to your brilliant argument? You are unlikely to be able to reply, which means that your opponent gets the last word and most importantly makes the final positive impression on the moot master.

While no one can ever guarantee that you will win a competition, if you follow this process you will be certainly be among the best prepared in the moot. Be better than ordinary. Find the answer that beats the initially best argument, then have the reply that beats that, and so on. You must always strive to beat your own best argument.

There is a flip side to this point that you need to think about. Just as people tend to stop at what they presume to be an obvious answer, they will ignore arguments they assume to be bad or weak ones. If you take the time to develop these arguments you will catch your opponents unawares. They will be left speechless and unprepared. It would not be unusual if your first really weak argument ultimately becomes your most effective!

A very significant advantage of undertaking step 5 is that it forces you to come up with innovative arguments. To beat seemingly impregnable arguments you need to investigate every single possible line of inquiry. This will often take you beyond the specific subject matter of the moot problem and into general areas of the field of law you are studying. This process increases your peripheral knowledge. Demonstrating this knowledge in answer to a moot master's question can often win you a moot.

This is only one possible approach you might take to developing your arguments. However, it is a very practical and very efficient method of tackling moot problems. Remember that most international competitions will require you to act for both sides at different stages of the moot. For example, in your first moot you may be representing the party bringing the claim, and in your second moot the party defending the claim. The suggested five-step approach effectively allows you to prepare the arguments for both sides simultaneously.

# Chapter 5

# Written documents

## MEMORANDA AND MEMORIALS

Most competitions require each team to submit a written document, although the form of documentation required can vary significantly. In some competitions, you are asked to provide a lengthy memorandum of submissions, sometimes called a memorial. On other occasions you need only submit a short outline of submissions, or you might be asked to prepare a case file. Although each of these different styles of written document serves a different function, they all have a similar purpose, that is, they force you to identify and deal with the relevant issues. Competitions that require documents of this kind will usually expect you to submit two documents, one for each side. The process of preparing the written documents doubles as an important step in the preparation of your oral presentations, hence it is worth preparing a written submission even where it is not required by the rules of the competition.

In some competitions, the written memorandum or memorial will form part of a document competition. Producing the document is usually the first task. Inevitably putting it together will involve considerable frustration, and immense pride once the task is completed.

Just as your team must decide on your commitment to the moot in terms of time and level of preparation, you must also decide how much effort you wish to put into the written documents. Obviously the more effort you put in, the better the documents you produce will be.

Documents from past years will usually be available on the competition website, and it is a sensible idea to obtain copies so that you can judge the standard. The standard will be very high, but you need not feel disheartened. Remember that this is a team activity and collectively your team will have the necessary skills.

# THE TIPS AND TRICKS OF WRITING

The task of producing the written documents for the moot task can be highly rewarding. It can also be difficult and frustrating, but with some thought and preparation your team can sail through this immensely satisfying aspect of the competition. This section examines some of the tips and tricks associated with memorandum writing.

## Knowing your purpose and your audience

The first thing you need to do is identify your purpose. Remember that you are not writing a scholarly dissertation. Although there are many similarities between a memorandum and a dissertation, and your research may be equivalent to that done by Masters students, your purpose is very different. Research dissertations seek to contribute or further scholarship, whereas you are simply arguing a case. Rather than analysing the law, you are applying the law. You are not being asked to discover a new legal doctrine, but to explain an existing one. Always reduce your task to its primary purpose. Keeping this in mind will help you produce a much better document.

If your purpose is not clear, and your document is beginning to resemble a dissertation, this will often be indicated by excessive referencing. Referencing is extremely important, and is covered on pages 29–30. However, it is possible to put too many references in a memorandum. Excessive referencing detracts from the document. It will not suggest that the weight of authority is on your side. It is more likely to be interpreted as "showing off" by those assessing the document.

The purpose of your written submission is to argue a fictional case before a panel of judges. These judges will be assessing only how well your document is written; they will not be determining whether your client wins or loses on the strength of your submission. In a moot competition you do not need to win the case to win a prize. This point is particularly important, and we return to it later in the context of oral submissions (see page 55).

You need to be pragmatic. Arguably, in a real case you are often under a duty to run every possible argument to advance your client's cause – although this too must be tempered. There is no such duty in a moot competition. The ideal document, which everyone should strive to create, will be one that also wins the case. But in a well-written moot problem, it is virtually impossible to create an ideal document. Moot problems are deliberately written to ensure that both sides have an arguable case. Furthermore, the problem will usually confine the issues to be discussed. Work within the parameters of the problem and to the expectations of your audience. This is what the judges will be looking for when they assess your document.

It is sometimes suggested that moot participants should not waste their time on weak arguments. For the reasons noted in step 5 of "Building an argument" (see pages 21–2), the effective presentation of weak arguments can often be a key to success. However, the advice is not entirely without merit. Your audience will have particular expectations. The readers of your document will expect to see certain arguments advanced and authorities cited. These are some of the prejudices any advocate faces when presenting a case. The safe path is not to disappoint your audience and to ensure you deal with the expected material. As you are likely to have a word or page limit, this may mean you are unable to cover all the arguments you have been developing in your document.

A good document will present the expected arguments, along with at least one or two unique arguments. These unique arguments are what will set your document apart. They must be developed carefully, and it is often easier to do this in a document rather than in an oral submission. Although ideally they should not need to, readers can flip backwards and forwards through your submission if necessary. This is not a luxury you have in an oral submission.

# Setting up your document

There are competition rules governing the length and presentation of the written memorandum. For example, you may be required to have a maximum of 35 pages with minimum right and left margins of 2.5 cm. Make sure you read these rules very carefully. If the page margin is defined in the rules, set the correct margins in your document even before you start writing.

As technology progresses, this otherwise time-consuming task is made easier and easier. Most students will have access to powerful word-processing programs. Learning how to fully utilise these programs will be of great benefit to you in your immediate task – that is, composing the written document – but also when completing research assignments and as you head out into the workforce. This section covers some of the important tools in your word-processing program that you will need to know how to use in order to compose your written document.

## Using styles

There are a number of functions in standard word-processing programs that you should learn before writing a single word. For example, you need to know how to "style" a document. This involves applying "style tags" to every paragraph and heading in your document. The style you apply to a paragraph will determine its font type and size, the margins, the line spacing and many other formatting features. This function allows you to have a consistent look to paragraphs and headings, without needing to go through every line and manually change the font or check margins. You can use the basic styles set-up in your word-processing program for a standard document, or you can create your own style names and give them the attributes you wish them to have. Before beginning to compose your document, work out what styles you will need. Typically you will need a standard paragraph style (probably numbered), and a different style for each level of heading in your document. This is very important for compiling a table of contents, which is discussed on page 28. You may also need a style for long quotes that are set separately from the running text.

The easiest way to create a new style is by adapting an existing one. If you do this, be very careful not to change the "Normal" style in your program. "Normal" is the name given to the base style in Microsoft Word. Other programs will have a similarly named style that performs the same function. It is the root of all other styles and should not be altered.

## Page numbering

A second function you should familiarise yourself with is page numbering. In some programs, it is simply a matter of selecting this option; in others you will need to insert a running foot. Both are straightforward processes. However, do you know how to change the page numbering style in the middle of the document? Or can you start numbering on page 5 of the electronic document? It is likely that you will need to do both.

As mentioned in the introduction to this section, there may be page limits placed on your document. It is also likely that according to the rules certain pages need not be included in that limit, for example, the table of contents or reference list. If this is the case, those pages should be numbered in a different way. You may decide to number pages that are not included in the page limit using Roman numerals. How this is done will vary from program to program, so you will need to investigate the process yourself. Typically it will involve dividing the document into sections.

## Cross-references

One of the most important and time-saving word-processing skills a lawyer will ever learn is how to automatically insert cross-references within a document. Lawyers are frequently called upon to draw up a contract and then, as negotiations progress, amend that contract several times. This may involve adding or removing paragraphs, and consequently the clause numbers will change. Each time this happens your document should be set to automatically amend any cross-references in other clauses. It is very poor risk management not to set up your document in this way, as it is easy for human editors to overlook the occasional cross-reference. While the consequences of cross-referencing mistakes in a moot document are certainly not as dire as in professional practice, it will detract from the overall impression of your document.

## Table of contents

Most word-processing programs have the capacity to create an automatically generated table of contents. This is another important use of the application of styles within your document. The automated table of contents function works very simply. It tells the computer to look for every paragraph styled as heading A, B and C, for example, and to list them along with their page number. The table of contents is generally the last thing you should create in your document.

## Avoiding common problems

There are some potential pitfalls in word-processing that you need to be aware of. A document that has been set up on one computer may look completely different on another computer. This is usually because a font you have chosen for one or more of the styles in your document may not be loaded on the other computer. As a result, the computer selects a replacement font for any missing fonts. This will affect the appearance of the text and the pagination. This problem is relatively easy to correct. You can load the fonts you need on the other computer, or use the original computer to print your document or check pagination. It is best to select commonly used fonts, such as Times New Roman and Palatino, to avoid this problem.

If the problem is more complex it may be harder to identify and correct. For example, your styles may be based on a particular style, the "Normal" style, for instance. You may have inadvertently and unknowingly set your style to automatically reflect any changes made to the "Normal" style. If the "Normal" style on computer 2 is different to that on computer 1, your document may look very different and may no longer comply with the rules. For example, it may now be 36 pages, rather than 35. This is a situation where team work is important. A good solution is to nominate one person to be the final writer on a designated computer.

A similar effect can occur when you cut and paste text from another document into your document. You may unintentionally import a new style into a document when you cut and paste. You can avoid this by pasting "Text only", without any formatting. For example, in Microsoft Word all the formatting features of a paragraph are contained in the hard return symbol "¶". If you highlight the text you wish to copy and paste, but do NOT highlight the paragraph symbol, you will be able to paste the text into your document without the unwanted formatting.

If you do need to print your document from computers other than the one on which it was created, you can avoid printing problems by saving it in PDF format. This should ensure that it will print from any computer.

## Referencing

Throughout your education you will have produced research essays, and you will be aware of the importance of proper referencing. It is especially important in the context of an international moot competition. There is a real possibility that one of the commentaries you refer to in your document has been delivered by one of the judges who is assessing your document. If you misquote, or worse plagiarise, the consequences will be dire.

There may be rules particular to your mooting competition about the form of referencing to be used. For example, you may not be allowed to use footnotes. It is vital that you know the referencing requirements before you begin your research. Using a referencing style involves not only knowing the correct form of citation, it also involves knowing how to compose your sentences in such a way that you can follow the referencing style correctly.

Those who commonly use footnotes or endnotes (often referred to as the Oxford style of referencing) may have some difficulty coming to terms with the Harvard system. If the referencing style is incorrectly applied, you could be referencing the application of a legal doctrine, rather than the legal doctrine itself. The consequence is that various authorities appear to be making a statement about the actual problem rather than about the law that applies to the problem.

## Being organised

In the course of preparing your arguments you are likely to read and consider more than 200 different articles or texts. It is impossible to remember the details of the relevant material from each of these texts. You need to write down the bibliographic details of any resource you read at the time you actually read the resource, not at the time you write the submission. Trying to pinpoint references for quotes in your document the night before it is due is not the best way to write a submission. Unless you take a proactive approach to referencing, you will need to devote considerable time once you have completed the rest of the document to correcting the referencing alone. No matter how well you prepare, you will always need to check the references in the final draft. This is an important task that should not be overlooked. However, there is a very big difference between checking references and correcting incomplete and inadequately prepared references. Make sure that you take an organised approach from the very beginning.

References are such a significant element in your final document, it may be worthwhile nominating one person in your team to be responsible for collecting references from other team members and maintaining a collective bibliography.

## Using bibliographic programs

Those of you who have had some experience with larger research projects may be familiar with bibliographic programs. These are programs specifically designed to help you manage your bibliographic references. They are essentially just databases. If you are unable to get access to one of the commercial products, it would be possible to achieve the same result from any standard database.

Databases operate by classifying information into specific fields. For example, for bibliographic references, the fields will include type of resource (book, journal article, internet, etc.), author's name, the title, and so on. By entering information in this way you are then able to determine how the information should be reproduced, and change it if needed. For example, you may need to present your references alphabetically listed by the name of the author, or you may wish to list them in date order. Having this option is important, because different referencing styles call for different methods of listing the information. The professional programs will have hundreds of different referencing options available for you to choose from. Select the one that complies with the rules of your competition and much of the hard work disappears, as your program will automatically set out your references in the required style.

## Using a proforma reference sheet

Irrespective of whether you are using a professional bibliographic program, a database you have created yourself, or just a list, it is very important that you give consideration to how you collect bibliographic information. Whoever is responsible for collating the references within the team will find it much easier to manage that information if it is presented in a standardised fashion. The easiest way to achieve this is to develop a proforma reference sheet. This sheet will identify the required information, such as author, title, type of resource and year of publication. Every team member should complete a new sheet for each reference that they read.

Although its primary function is for referencing purposes, with very minor amendments the reference sheet can be a valuable tool in other ways. For example, the person completing the sheet may be asked to rate the resource out of five, provide a summary or identify key words. This information will be very useful to other team members if you decide to rotate research areas. Key words can be used by those writing the document to quickly identify resources that are relevant to the section they are currently working on. If you are keeping any kind of electronic record of these reference sheets, running a key word search will be very easy.

Here is an example of a referencing sheet that you can copy or adapt to your team's needs.

**Title:** _____

_____

*(Article title / chapter title / case name)*

**Publication name:** _____

_____

*(Journal title / book title)*

**Web address:** _____

_____

**First author:** _____

*(First name / SURNAME)*

**Second author:** _____

*(First name / SURNAME)*
*Any other authors should be noted in bold in*
*'General comments' below*

**Date viewed:** _____

**Date (year) published:** _____

**Publisher:** _____

_____

**ISSN / ISBN:**

**Citation:**

**Pages:**

*(Official journal citation / Case citations – all available in proper hierarchy)*

**Rating (1 poor – 5 excellent):**

**Countries referred to:**

**Select appropriate key words:**

*(Determine a list of key words relevant to your topic.)*

**Other:** *(key words not in list)*

**General comments:**

*(This should include a brief summary of main arguments / points raised. Attach more paper if required.)*

**NAME:**

*(It is important to know who completed the sheet.)*

# Writing style

The documents produced by your team need to be written in a clear, consistent, flowing style. This will assist readers of your document to follow the logic of your arguments and understand your case.

## Achieving 'one voice'

We each have our own distinctive writing style. There may be simple phrases that we tend to repeat, and particular ways we construct a paragraph. It is very easy to recognise when different passages in one document have been written by different people. In order to achieve consistency and fluency in your team's work, it is important that your document has a uniform style or "one voice". There are several ways this can be achieved while still ensuring that each member of the team contributes.

The simplest method is to delegate writing to particular team members. This may be one or several people. If several people are chosen, then those people should write together. This means that as far as possible they should all be sitting in front of the same keyboard as the document is produced. Other team members will be responsible for bringing the research and arguments to be transformed into the written document. In this way the writers are the scribes whose job is to translate the ideas of the whole group into one document.

Delegating the writing to a group of several people can lead to problems. One of the underlying themes of this book is the need to think about what you are going to do before you actually do it. Give some thought to the difficulties that may arise when several team members are acting as scribes and identify ways to avoid them.

Writing with one voice will not only improve your document but it is also a very important exercise in learning how to work together as a team. Those members of the team who do the research for the writers will sometimes face the difficult task of seeing their arguments written in different ways. If you are in this position, there may be times when you find your arguments so transformed that they are barely recognisable. How you respond to this situation will have a considerable effect on both the unity and smooth functioning of the whole team. Whatever role you are in, you are handing over some of the responsibility for the outcome to others, which requires you to have faith in your team-mates. The writers must remember that they are being entrusted to prepare a group document, and should not let their own personal ideas overpower ideas from the rest of the team.

## Presenting information to the team scribes

The team needs to think about how the researchers should present information to the writers in order to minimise potential difficulties. The information can be presented orally or in writing.

Set rules about how written information should be presented. For example, you might want to list key or fundamental points that must be reflected in the document at the top of the page. Underneath these, you could provide an explanation of these points for the benefit of the writers. Unless they are confident that the explanation fits the voice of the document as a whole, the writers should resist the temptation to simply cut and paste these explanations into the document. Quotes and references should also be clearly identified. Determining a standard approach that everyone understands will avoid pitfalls such as the writers omitting a key point. If the research is presented in a standardised way, with the key points clearly identified, then those points cannot be overlooked.

This technique has a very close parallel in professional legal practice. When you begin legal practice you will almost certainly be asked to do research for a more senior lawyer. Usually, this research will be presented in the form of a memorandum, and most firms will have a guide as to how the memorandum should be structured.

The oral presentation of information is really just a discussion between the researchers and the writers. It allows the researchers to explain in more detail the importance and significance of the research they are providing. It is also a time when researchers can comment on what the writers have actually written. However, researchers should not be allowed to completely rewrite passages in the document. One way to ensure this cannot happen is to have a rule that only writers are allowed to type into the actual document. Researchers should be given a hard copy of any relevant section of the document to comment on, criticise and edit, but they should not directly edit the master document.

# Structuring your document

One of the secrets of a good document, and for that matter an argument generally, is to ensure that it flows logically from point to point. It is not possible to simply sit down and write a flawless document – considerable planning is required. Just as you might follow a map in order to go somewhere new, you need to map out a framework for your document.

One way to do this is to put your ideas on a whiteboard. An advantage of using a whiteboard is that it is very easy to change the structure of your ideas until you find the best approach. Another method is to use a large piece of paper, or put each of your ideas on an ordinary sheet of paper and spread them out over the floor or attach them to a board. It can be very helpful to use a digital camera during this process. Taking a photo of your framework is a simple way of recording your work.

Planning your approach is not unique to moot competitions. It is extremely important in other aspects of your studies, such as in examinations. A good examination tip is to spend a few moments drawing a quick map of your anticipated answer before you begin. Not only does this help you stay focused when you are writing the answer, but also serves to guide the examiner through your answer. If you run out of time in an exam, the concept map you have drawn should demonstrate that you know how to answer the question, and often examiners will take that into account when awarding marks.

## Headings and paragraphs

Within your document you will need to guide the reader through your submissions. This is commonly done through the use of headings, where each distinct section of your material is presented with its own heading. Some competitions outline specific headings that must be used, whereas others allow you to determine your own. Ineffective headings will detract from the document as a whole, and obscure the underlying structure of your argument. As a consequence you need to take great care when composing your headings.

A heading must clearly express the theme of the paragraphs that follow. It should be from your client's perspective, and ideally it will be short and concise. Different level headings must be used in a consistent manner. You must not only ensure that headings of the same level are formatted in the same way, but that their relative significance and importance are consistent within your heading hierarchy.

Well-constructed paragraphs also play an important role. Paragraphs delineate issues for a reader. They also break up information into consumable parts. While there is no set length for a paragraph, it should not be particularly long. Each paragraph should contain a topic sentence. This is usually but not necessarily the first sentence. The topic sentence briefly introduces the point of the paragraph. There should only be one main point per paragraph. The middle sentences of a paragraph develop and provide evidence for the point being made. It is important that the final sentence is not simply a repeat of the topic sentence, as this will give your reader the feeling that the paragraph is going round in circles. The final sentence should reiterate the point by drawing on the evidence provided by the middle sentences.

## Avoiding contradictory arguments

A well-structured document will take a reader step by step to the conclusion you want them to reach. Frequently you will do this by presenting a series of alternative routes: if the reader does not accept your first argument, then you have another argument to follow that supports your case.

A common trap is to present contradictory arguments rather than alternative ones. Contradictory arguments suggest that there may be a flaw in your case, whereas numerous alternative arguments will lead the reader to conclude that the outcome you are proposing is indeed the correct one. How your document is structured will often affect whether an argument appears to be contradictory or a positive alternative. This typically occurs where you have mutually exclusive arguments.

Mutually exclusive arguments are ones that cannot co-exist – that is, they are contradictory. In other words, if your reader accepts proposition A, they must by definition reject proposition B. Often situations like these will be immediately apparent, while in other situations the conflict may be initially obscured by the different levels of argument presented.

This can be demonstrated by reference to a relatively simple example. The example that follows relates to arbitration law, but the principles apply to any area of law and in any dispute forum.

In this example, the parties involved have agreed to have their dispute resolved by arbitration. The arbitration is to take place in Australia. The law governing the contract was not expressly stated and is now in issue. The New Zealand based Respondent wants to argue that English law governs the contract. New Zealand's conflict of law rules point to the application of English law.

As Australia is the place of the arbitration, we must first look at Australian law. Australia has adopted the UNCITRAL Model Law.

Article 28 of the UNCITRAL Model Law is as follows:

### Rules applicable to the substance of the dispute

*(1) The arbitral tribunal shall decide the dispute in accordance with such rules of law as are chosen by the parties as applicable to the substance of the dispute. Any designation of the law or legal system of a given State shall be construed, unless otherwise expressed, as directly referring to the substantive law of that State and not to its conflict of laws rules.*

*(2) Failing any designation by the parties, the arbitral tribunal shall apply the law determined by the conflict of laws rules which it considers applicable.*

The Respondent believes it can make two submissions. It can argue that pursuant to the New Zealand conflict of law rules English law will apply; or it can argue that there was an implied agreement between the parties that English law would apply. The order in which these two arguments are presented will affect whether they are contradictory or simply put in the alternative.

The Respondent presented the arguments as follows:

*The Respondent submits that this Tribunal should apply the conflict of laws rules of New Zealand under Article 28(2) of the UNCITRAL Model Law to find that English law governs this contract. It makes this submission because …*

*Alternatively, this Tribunal should find that the parties have chosen the laws of England to apply under Article 28(1) of the UNCITRAL Model Law.*

The arguments may have been placed in this order because the Respondent believed the implied agreement argument was the weaker one. There is a presumption that you should lead with your best argument, but despite the fact that both arguments arrive at the same conclusion, presented in this fashion they are contradictory.

The reason the arguments are contradictory when presented this way is because Article 28 UNCITRAL Model Law requires the Tribunal to first look to the parties' agreement, and then to apply conflict of laws rules only if the parties have not made any agreement. By first arguing that the Tribunal should apply the conflict of laws rules of New Zealand, the Respondent is in essence accepting that the parties have not made a choice of law. The Respondent contradicts itself by then arguing the parties chose the laws of England to apply.

If, however, the order of the submissions were reversed the Respondent would have two logically coherent alternative arguments. The Respondent should first ask the Tribunal to find an implied agreement. It is only in the event that the Tribunal does not accept the submission that it needs to even consider the second. We can call these "cascading alternatives".

# Basic rules of writing

There are many good books available that set out the basic rules of writing. A number of these are listed in Part 2. You are strongly encouraged to borrow some of these books from your library.

Those students who are native English speakers will have probably already learnt these rules, although it never hurts to revisit them. Indeed, this may be where non-native English speakers have an advantage. Upon returning home from international mooting competitions, some native English-speaking participants have remarked with some embarrassment on the fact that the non-native speakers spoke better English than they did.

The same is true of the documents. A quick review of the document awards for the Vis Moot reveals that only twice in the history of the competition has a native English-speaking team won first prize for a document. All other first-prize winners have been non-native speakers. No doubt there are many reasons for this, however complacency is probably one of the biggest factors. People from any country can become lazy when conversing in their native tongue, and are more likely to lapse into slang and colloquial expressions. Abbreviated forms of expression, such as "g'day" for "good day" have evolved simply because we are too lazy to enunciate the complete words.

Similarly, we tend to become lazy when applying the general rules of writing in our own language. If you want to do well in the document competition, you cannot afford to do this. While it is not within the scope of this book to examine all these rules in detail, there are a number of rules that are particularly pertinent to written advocacy.

## Sentence construction

Writing that is intended to be argumentative and assertive should be written in the "active voice". Sentences should follow the sequence: subject, verb, object. If you place the subject at the beginning of the sentence, you give it emphasis. You should then place the verb directly after the subject without any intervening words if possible. The object should then closely follow the verb. Sentences written in the active voice tend to be short and direct, which is perfect for your task.

The Respondent breached its duty.

There may be occasions where you deliberately want to understate something, for example, when presenting a weak argument. In these situations it might be appropriate for you to use the "passive voice". The passive voice reverses the position of the subject and object in the sentence: object, verb, subject. These sentences tend to be longer than active voice sentences.

The duty was breached by the Respondent.

Whether you are using the active or passive voice, it is important to construct your sentences so that the order of the words does not create ambiguity. You need to take particular care with the placement of any modifiers in the sentence. A modifier is a word or phrase that gives extra information about another word or phrase. Consider the following example.

The food aid was ruined on the date it was received by the Parthian refugee agency.

In this sentence, the modifier is the phrase "by the Parthian refugee agency". It is not clear whether the agency is doing the receiving, or the ruining, or both, therefore the sentence should be recast to remove the ambiguity.

In complex sentences where there are multiple subjects and verbs, it is wise to present verbs in the same form to avoid confusion. For example, in the following sentence, inserting the second 'is' helps the reader to understand the sentence easily.

The Respondent **is** responsible for the maintenance of the satellite and **is** liable for the damage it caused.

## Using words appropriately

Your ability to select the appropriate words is naturally limited to the extent of your vocabulary, or in the case of your team your collective vocabulary. Native speakers of a language often have a natural advantage in this regard as they tend to have a larger vocabulary than non-native speakers of a language.

However, both native and non-native English speakers can fall into the trap of mismatching words. A common mistake is using an inappropriate verb with a noun. A mismatch of this sort leads to subjects doing things they cannot actually do. For example, a court may "find" or "rule" or "determine", but it cannot "submit".

The following example is incorrect:

In the shipping case *The Poseidon*, the Court submitted . . .

The correct form would be:

In the shipping case *The Poseidon*, the Court found . . .

The subject and verb in a sentence must always agree in number. This means that a singular subject needs a singular verb, and similarly a plural subject requires a plural verb. It can be easy to spot cases where subjects and verbs disagree in number, but it becomes more difficult in sentences where a phrase has been inserted between the subject and verb, particularly if the phrase includes a noun that differs in number from the subject of the sentence. The rule is that the verb must agree with the subject, not with any intervening noun.

The Applicant's submission, although purportedly supported by all those authorities, is misconceived.

If your sentence has two nouns joined by the word "and", you should use a plural verb. You would use a singular verb if the sentence contained two singular nouns that are joined by "or". If there are both singular and plural nouns joined by "or", the verb should agree with the nearest noun.

The following constructions are correct.

The Applicant and the Respondent are responsible.
The Applicant or the Respondent is responsible.
The Applicant or the Respondents are responsible.
The Applicants or the Respondent is responsible.

## Avoid gender-specific language

As a consequence of now antiquated social norms, the use of masculine pronouns developed as the default form of expression when giving general examples. This has been rightly criticised, and many official legal documents such as statutes must be written in gender-neutral language. Indeed, it is also a rule of most moot competitions.

A common difficulty arises when you need to use a singular pronoun in a general example. For example, "Each member of counsel must present his (or her) documents". The pronouns "his" and "her" are obviously gender specific and should be avoided unless you are referring to a particular person. In some cases, it is possible to use "its" although this can sometimes seem clumsy. A way of circumventing this problem is by using a plural pronoun such as "their", which is gender neutral. Technically this is grammatically incorrect if the noun referred to by the pronoun is singular, however it does seem to be used with increasing regularity.

If possible, it is better to rephrase the sentence to avoid the problem altogether. You can either recast the sentence so that a pronoun is not needed, or you make both the original noun and pronoun plural. (The example above would become: "Members of counsel must present their documents.")

## Keep the tense consistent

The tense used in a sentence provides a timeframe for the action that is being described. There are twelve main tenses in the English language. If you write in the active voice, as described above, you are very unlikely to encounter more than a few different tenses. The "simple" tenses, as they are referred to, are the most commonly used and easiest to understand. The simple tenses are past, present and future.

The Applicant submitted . . . (past tense)
The Applicant submits . . . (present tense)
The Applicant will submit . . . (future tense)

Two other common tenses are the "past perfect" and "present perfect". You use the past perfect tense to refer to something that happened before the action you are now describing.

The Applicant had submitted . . . (past perfect tense)

The present perfect tense is used when an action is continuing, that is, it began in the past but is ongoing, or where the action occurred at an indefinite time in the past.

The Applicant has submitted . . . (present perfect tense)

As the above examples demonstrate, the "past" and "present perfect" tenses can be used to convey a similar meaning. The most important rule about tenses is not to change tense in the middle of a sentence. The tense you use should remain consistent throughout your document. The need for consistency applies to many different aspects of the preparation and presentation of your document.

# Editing

Editing is an invaluable part of the preparation of any document. It is inevitable that you will make errors while writing the first draft of your submission. When you consider the complexity of the writing process, this is not surprising. When you write, you are not simply thinking about the next word that is about to appear, you are thinking about the whole sentence. You are also thinking about the point you are making in the paragraph as a whole, so you are thinking about the sentences that are to come as well as those you have already written. You might have external distractions as well, such as the presence of other team members. With all of this going on, it is little wonder that sometimes the ideas you have in your head are not conveyed perfectly by the words you write on the page.

Editing allows you to compensate for these distractions. Once you have written your first draft, print it out and read it carefully and as objectively as you can. Although some people feel comfortable reading documents on a computer screen, there is a risk associated with editing in this way. Authors of documents have a tendency to read what they intended to write, not necessarily what has actually been written. There is likely to be a greater risk of doing this if you read the document on the screen.

When learning to study, students are often encouraged to have a dedicated space where all they do is study. We train ourselves that if we are sitting in that seat we are there to work. A psychological association is formed. The same can occur when writing submissions, whether as part of a moot competition or for a real case. For this reason, when you begin the editing process it is a good idea to find a place to work in that is different from where the document was written. This can help you clear your mind for the task ahead.

The aim when editing is to be as objective as possible. Try to read the document as if you were reading it for the first time. Apart from correcting spelling and grammatical errors, you should also ensure that each sentence serves a purpose and makes sense. One way of doing this is to read the document aloud. Sometimes hearing your ideas out loud will prompt you to notice something you missed when reading it silently to yourself. Be brutally honest with yourself. Sometimes thoughts do not translate well into sentences and paragraphs. The idea might be good, but the expression of it in your document may not be clear or logically set out. If you identify a passage like this, simply rewrite is so that it better conveys your idea. This is exactly why we go through the editing process.

Regardless of how hard you try to be objective when editing your own work, it will be impossible for you to be totally objective. It is essential to have someone else also edit the document. You can ask another member of your team, and you can also ask a family member or a friend.

Another member of your team who has not been involved in the writing process will have a greater level of objectivity, as well as an understanding of the substantive content of the document. This person can advise on matters of expression as well as the content.

Having a family member or friend look at your document, one who has no idea about what you are writing, can offer you different benefits. First, this person will be even more objective than your team-mates. Like you, other team members will have a tendency to read words that are not there because they are familiar with the material. Second, and perhaps most importantly, if this person can understand your argument then you know you have expressed it clearly and logically. If your submission appeals to both those who know about the law and those who do not, then it is likely to do well.

# THE SECOND DOCUMENT

In most competitions you are expected to submit written submissions for both sides, that is, the party bringing the claim and the party defending the claim. Some competitions, such as the Jessup Moot, require these documents to be submitted on the same date. Other competitions, such as the Vis Moot, call for the second document at a later stage. In the latter situation, you will probably receive another competitor's document to which you must respond. From a participant's perspective, there is relatively little substantive difference between the two approaches. The method for developing and constructing your arguments will work equally well. Time and task allocation will be the most significant practical considerations.

However, it is likely that this will be your first chance to see what other teams have been doing. Ideally, the docmuent they have produced will be along the same lines as yours, but it is possible that it will be quite different. If it is, sit back and critically evaluate your own work in comparison to the document you have received. Be as objective as you can about which document has adopted the better approach. If you decide the other document is better, do not spend time worrying about the document you have already completed. Most competitions expect that the arguments advanced by students in the oral stages of the competition will have developed significantly since the submission of the written documents. Learn from what you have received, and work hard on producing a really good second document.

## Preparing a genuine response

It is important to remember that you must provide a response to your opponent's submission. Your preparation may lead you to the false presumption that you can write the responding document without even looking at the submissions of your opponent. This is simply not true and would be tactically very unwise.

Read and consider your opponent's arguments carefully. They may be subtly different to your own. Demonstrate to the reader that you have done this by referring specifically to passages in your opponent's document. Examine the way they have interpreted authorities. Can you challenge these interpretations? Take great care to address all the specific submissions raised.

## Is it good or bad to get a 'weak' memorandum to respond to?

There are three sorts of documents you are likely to receive. The first is a weak document. The second is one that you believe is roughly on par with the document you submitted. The third is a document that you believe is even stronger than yours.

You might instinctively think that it is advantageous to receive a weak document. You would be wrong! Do not misunderstand the nature of the competition. A responding document will not win a prize simply because it is better than the first document. Just like the first document, it is being judged principally on content. The second document has the added complexity of needing to respond to the first document, and naturally this plays a very important role in a document's ultimate success or failure. However, it is rarely, if ever, a determining factor.

It follows then that the best type of document to receive is a really strong one. A strong document is more likely to challenge you to produce a strong reply. If the arguments it raises are new to you, you will now be aware of them and will be forced to respond. Responding will be easier, as the points will be presented in a logical way, which in turn will allow you to respond in a similar way.

Documents that are of a similar standard are generally more comforting than helpful. Replying to a document of this kind is probably the least intensive, and requires less work than responding to strong or weak documents.

Responding to a weak document is the most difficult. A weak document is generally one that has very little substance, or the argument is very hard to understand. This can be due to language difficulties or just simply poor construction. Whatever the cause of the weakness in the document, you now face problems. In the first situation, do you respond to issues that are not there but you believe should be? In the second situation, how do you respond tactfully?

## Do you respond to issues that your opponent missed?

The competition rules and other information provided by the competition organisers will generally provide guidance on this issue. In the absence of such advice, it is best to assume that you should respond to issues that your opponent has missed. The challenge is to tactfully yet clearly distinguish where you respond to the actual arguments raised by your opponent from your response to the arguments you believe they should have raised.

It is important that you do not lose your focus. Always act positively in strengthening your case. Attempt to discredit your opponent's case, never your opponent personally. One way to do this is to address concerns that you believe your reader may have. For example, you might say, "This Honourable Court may be concerned that the letter of 12 May 2001 was not a valid notice of avoidance." This approach can be very convincing because it demonstrates that you have thought very carefully about your case. It shows that you have identified areas that might be perceived as weaknesses and have addressed them. However, most importantly, you are making your point with a measured degree of subtlety. There is no attempt to embarrass your opponent; instead you are buttressing your client's position.

## How do you respond tactfully?

Do not be distracted by any weakness you might perceive in counsel for the other side. Always treat them with the highest respect. As the saying goes, play the ball and not the person. If you play the person, it will not advance your document in any way and is very likely to be considered a violation of the spirit of the competition, potentially resulting in penalties.

The key is to focus on presenting a positive case on behalf of your client. Adopting this approach also guards against complacency.

Although you write your response believing that it is the best effort your opponent could muster, you should immediately adopt the opposite opinion as soon as the document is submitted.

Competitions that have a two-stage document program generally make the documents a precondition of participation. In other words, if you fail to submit the first document you are out of the competition. Some teams will face difficult timing issues, and may have very little time to submit the first document. In these cases rather than drop out of the competition, teams will not concern themselves with the first document competition and simply submit whatever they have at the due date. As a consequence, you should draw no conclusions about a team's ability to perform in the oral stages of the competition from the quality of their document. It is commonplace that you will face the team you are responding to in the oral stages. Do not be lulled into a false sense of security or make assumptions about the quality of your opponents' advocacy.

## THE OUTLINE OF SUBMISSIONS

This section is intended to include all documents that summarise the submissions. Depending on the competition it may be referred to as an "outline of submissions", a "summary of argument" or even just "submissions". Although there are likely to be subtle differences between them regarding presentation, they are all relatively short documents.

In contrast to memorials and memoranda, referred to above, an outline of submissions is typically only a few pages long. The underlying purpose of the document, to provide a structure and explanation of your case, remains the same, but the level of detail is different.

An outline of submissions needs to identify all the authorities on which you intend to rely. You would usually state the proposition you intend to make and then simply list the cases in support. As a consequence there is generally only a couple of sentences per paragraph.

Many of the strategies for writing a memorandum or memorial apply equally to writing an outline of submissions. In particular, you should implement the strategies discussed in the section entitled "Structuring your document" (pages 36–9). As in a memorial or memorandum, you must ensure that your alternative arguments are genuine alternatives. You should write in the active voice. You should edit your outline of submissions. These are all very important steps in the process. Even though you may not be entering a document competition, the moot masters will read your written work. Indeed, they are likely to see your outline of submissions quite some time before they see you, which means that your outline of submissions will create the first impression. Make sure their first impression is a good one.

# THE CASEBOOK

The casebook, sometimes referred to as an "appeal book", "case file" or "trial notebook", is a mini reference library. Every authority, whether it be a case or a commentary, that you intend to refer to during your submission should be reproduced in the casebook. In a real case the parties are often directed to jointly agree on and prepare the contents of the casebook. This cooperation is unlikely to occur in a moot competition, purely because of the time constraints involved.

International moot competitions do not commonly require that casebooks be compiled and submitted; however, having one can be a considerable advantage. Frequently you will want to cite a particular passage from a judgment or commentary. If you are in a position to quote that passage for the moot master, it will demonstrate your level of preparedness. It is particularly impressive when you are able to quote an authority in response to an argument raised by your opponent, especially if you can demonstrate that your opponent is misconstruing the authority.

How the casebook is composed requires thought. It must be functional. If it takes you longer than three seconds to find a particular document in your casebook, it is not functional. There must be a logical and immediately apparent system to the ordering of your authorities. It must be immediately apparent because others may also be using the casebook. If the competition specifically requires a casebook, you should be prepared to provide one to both the moot masters and your opponents. Always have a couple of copies of your casebook to hand in case you are asked to provide them, but unless asked you do not need to volunteer a copy.

There are a number of logical sequences that you might consider. You may collate the authorities alphabetically. Although this is logical it is not ideal. There are too many variables. For example, if you are including a commentary, should it be listed under the title or the author's name? A better approach is to order the references in the sequence you intend to refer to them. Separate each reference with a divider and tab, then number each tab. This is a very straightforward and effective method.

However, it is not enough though to set the order once and then just blindly follow it thereafter. You need to develop an awareness of where all your references are in the casebook. You need to know which decision of the International Court of Justice is under tab number 3, for example. Without this knowledge you may get into difficulty if the moot masters take you away from your intended structure. The way to learn these skills is discussed in the section headed "Using case materials" below (see pages 77–9).

# Chapter 6

# Oral submissions

While only some moots have a document competition, all moots have oral hearings. The style and rules of the competitions vary greatly. For example, in most moots you stand to make your submissions, but in an arbitration moot you usually make your presentation sitting down. It is very important that you have researched the rules governing how your moot is to be conducted. You need to feel comfortable in the moot environment. The less stressed you feel the better your performance will be. Familiarising yourself with the process, thereby reducing the possibility of surprises, is an important step in reducing stress.

As you read this section on producing oral submissions, consider how many of the techniques discussed can be traced back to one fundamental task – thinking about thinking. How often do you think about how you actually think through a problem and understand concepts and arguments? For example, do you think in pictures or in words? Some people find understanding a concept much easier if they can see the concept represented as a diagram. Others tend to think in words. Everyone is unique, although the differences may only be a matter of degree.

When you present an argument, you need to recognise that your audience may have different ways of understanding the presentation of your argument. No one in your audience will think in exactly the same way as you. As a consequence, your carefully constructed plan that makes perfect sense to you may not make sense to someone else.

Whatever the context in which the communication of ideas is taking place – whether you are presenting a submission in a moot court, delivering a speech or making a point in a tutorial – you need to make sure that your points will be effectively and efficiently understood by your audience. The responsibility for this is borne both by you and your audience, and will depend on the occasion and the nature of the communication. If you are presenting to a large group, such a class, then the class members have to individually assimilate the information in a manner that is most effective and efficient for them. However, you as the presenter should arm them with the ability to do this by briefly explaining the basis of your thinking on the topic. When you are acting as an advocate in the smaller environment of a moot competition or courtroom, you must bear more of the responsibility and adapt to the needs of the audience.

To demonstrate this point consider the following diagram.

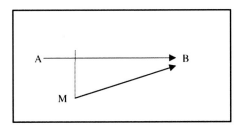

The box-shaped border represents the boundaries of the moot problem. During your thorough preparation you have examined every single point within the box. After careful consideration you have decided that to win your case you must reach point B. You believe that the most effective and efficient way to do this is to go in a straight line from point A. In your mind this path represents the shortest series of logical steps that can be taken to achieve your objective. However, your moot masters are unlikely to have explored the problem in exactly the same way as you and therefore will have a different level of knowledge. They will not have spent the same amount of time preparing and researching the case. As a consequence they will not necessarily share your view of the best path. This can be usually and quickly identified by the questions asked by the moot masters. In the diagram, point M represents a question asked by the moot master. This provides a different starting point for the problem than the one you chose. You still need to find the most effective and efficient path to point B but this time starting from point M, so you will need to adapt your submission. Resist the temptation to return strictly to your earlier path as it will result in a less effective submission than one that has been adapted in response to the moot master's questions.

# HOW TO STRUCTURE AN ORAL SUBMISSION

The ideal oral submission is one in which you are always in complete control. You take your moot masters on a step-by-step journey to the conclusion you want them to reach. You control how the issues are framed. You control what and when questions are asked. Sound impossible? It is difficult and a challenge, but it is by no means impossible. The keys to success are preparation and practice. It certainly helps if you have a charismatic presence, but good preparation will always beat charisma alone.

## Making a start

If you have gone through the process covered earlier in the section entitled "Building an argument" (pages 18–22), you will already have done substantial preparation. You will have already done the work necessary to ensure you are in command of the subject matter of the moot. This section of the book discusses how to put all that work into a convincing oral submission.

The first step is to be aware of the environment in which you are making your submission. The second step is to identify your aim and purpose, which will help you determine the overall structure of your submission. The principles that apply to preparing an oral submission for a moot competition will also apply to preparation for a real court or arbitration hearing.

Find out how much time has been allocated for you to make your presentation. While fixed-time presentations are most commonly found in moots, they are certainly not uncommon in arbitrations, and are becoming increasingly seen in courts. Be aware of any time limits and ensure that you work within them.

Finally, remember that it is not necessary to win the case to win the moot.

## Dealing with the expectations of moot masters

A moot problem is a limited dispute with expectations. It is a limited dispute partly to ensure that participants focus on a particular area of law or issue, and partly to ensure that everyone is ultimately arguing the same point. In those competitions where you do not have any contact with other competitors until the oral hearings, it is particularly important that everyone is dealing with the same issues. Everyone who reads the moot problem should be aware of the boundaries within which competitors are expected to argue, and this includes your moot masters.

The area of law at the centre of the moot problem arouses expectations in the minds of those who will be judging you in the competition. These expectations were referred to earlier as prejudices or bias on the part of the moot masters, because they have preconceived ideas about the arguments that should be run. Moot masters are more likely to think that there is something wrong with your submission if the arguments they expect to hear are not covered. This is particularly true of those competitions that direct you to particular cases and resources in the official documentation. Do not let this prevent you from coming up with innovative arguments. On the contrary, simply be aware of the hurdles you face – any prejudice can be overcome.

You need to know who the moot masters are and bear this in mind when preparing your submission. This too will vary significantly from competition to competition. The moot masters may be eminent judges and jurists, experienced practitioners in the relevant field, legal academics, or coaches of other teams. If you are appearing before a panel, you may encounter masters from a range of legal traditions. Your challenge is to develop a submission that will appeal and impress every type of moot master, although of course you can only predict what these expectations might be. We will return to this topic in the context of practice moots (see pages 87–9).

# Creating a persuasive case
## Express your case in the simplest possible terms

Although the arguments and points of law upon which you want to rely may be quite complex, it is important that you express them as simply as possible. The simple case will appeal to the majority of people. To begin the simple case, start with a short and concise statement of the crux of your submission. Here is an example.

> The Appellant has suffered loss because of the Respondent's wrongful avoidance of the contract.

This is a strong opening that leaves the audience in no doubt about the direction of your submissions.

## Use 'signposting'

You should then break down the assertion into its constituent parts.

> On behalf of the Appellant I will be addressing the wrongful avoidance of the contract, and my co-counsel will address the entitlement to damages.
>
> The Appellant's submissions on wrongful avoidance are made in three parts. One, there has not been a fundamental breach by the Appellant that would allow avoidance. Two, even if the breach was fundamental the Appellant had validly exercised its right to cure thereby preventing avoidance. Three, in any event the Respondent has failed to give the obligatory notice. Each of these arguments is made in the alternative. This Honourable Court need only accept one of these submissions to find that the Respondent wrongfully avoided the contract.

This paragraph demonstrates the use of several techniques that should be utilised throughout the entire submission. First, each separate part the advocate intends to address is clearly identified and listed. The numerical references are important. Numbers, particularly small numbers, are understood by everyone. By associating each aspect of the submission with a number, the advocate makes it easier for the Court to follow the submission. It is a technique that is often referred to as "signposting". Signposting is very important in an oral presentation. In essence, signposting is simply providing an outline of your arguments.

This technique has a number of advantages. With a written sub-mission, a reader can look back through earlier pages if necessary. However, during an oral submission, your audience will need to rely on their memory (or note-taking ability) to recall what was said in the earlier parts of your submission. As a consequence you want your audience to be thinking forwards not backwards. Describing where you intend to take your audience naturally shifts their atten-tion forwards towards that destination.

Second, by giving your audience the broad structure of your submission at the beginning you will make it much easier for them to follow the progression of your arguments. You enable your audience to immediately satisfy themselves that there is a prima facie logic to your argument. Their focus then shifts from your overall argument to the detail of your argument. They will now simply be considering whether each successive point follows.

Finally, and this follows on from the second point, you take the guesswork out of your submission, leaving your audience free to concentrate on what you are saying. You are in control of how the issue will progress. Your audience is not distracted by wondering which way your argument will go. The audience knows exactly what you are going to do and how you intend to do it.

## Offer alternative arguments

The example above showed the technique of offering alternatives. This is an example of the "cascading alternatives" we discussed on pages 37–9. They are genuinely alternative (not contradictory) arguments, and each successive argument need only be considered if the earlier ones are rejected. It is not necessary to explain their cascading nature at this stage of the presentation, as it is often a useful segue between alternatives.

In any form of advocacy, your intention is to persuade your audience to reach a particular conclusion. One way of doing this is to make it easy for your audience to reach that conclusion. Presenting a variety of alternative arguments makes both your task and the audience's task a lot easier. As the saying goes, all roads lead to Rome, and this is what you are telling your audience: it does not matter which path you take, you will end up at my conclusion.

## Address alternative submissions

After outlining the three alternative submissions, the advocate then addresses each one.

> Beginning with the Applicant's first and primary submission, there has not been a fundamental breach. To establish fundamental breach the Respondent must prove: one, that there was a breach; two, that the breach caused such detriment to the Respondent as to substantially deprive it of what it was entitled to expect. The Applicant will not be making any submissions on the issue of mere breach, rather it will be focusing on the lack of substantial detriment. It is important to note that the burden of proof lies with the Respondent. It is not up to the Applicant to convince the Court of either of the points; that responsibility lies with the Respondent. If the Respondent fails to satisfactorily prove to this Honourable Court either of these two elements, it naturally follows that there was not a fundamental breach and consequently wrongful avoidance.
>
> Turning to the issue of substantial detriment . . .

This example demonstrates further techniques that can be very compelling when you are responding to or defending a claim: setting the hurdles for the opposition, outlining where the opposition bears the burden of proof, and selecting your argument.

It stands to reason that if you are trying to make it easy for your audience to agree with you, you also want to make it hard for the audience to agree with your opponent. This can be done by singling out and emphasising each element of your opponent's case. It is very important that you show that these elements are not alternatives. Explain to the audience that for the opposition's case to succeed, they must prove every single element. By doing this you are placing a number of hurdles in front of your opposition. You also have the tactical advantage of establishing the battleground. Some issues will naturally favour your client and they should be exploited.

Once you have set out as many elements as possible, you should emphasise where the other side bears the burden of proof. This is particularly useful because it defines both your task and that of your opponent. If your opponent has the burden of proof then they must satisfy the moot masters to the requisite standard (for example, on the balance of probabilities, or beyond reasonable doubt). Your submissions are not measured by the same standard. In a strict sense, even if you did not make any submissions your opponent could fail to meet their burden. However, normally you would make submissions but these need only create sufficient doubt. Without overdoing it, you can gain an advantage by reminding your audience of this repeatedly throughout your submission.

Although you would normally make submissions where your opponent bears the burden of proof, it can be a good idea not to make submissions on extremely weak points. In the example above, the advocate elected not to make submissions on whether or not there was a breach, instead choosing to focus on the presence or otherwise of substantial detriment. Choosing not to make submissions on a point is not the same as admitting that point. The other side will still bear the burden of proving it. This approach is often referred to as putting the other side to their proof, and is particularly useful where you have limited time. It allows you to spend more time concentrating on and explaining the arguments that are advantageous to your case, rather than wasting time on weak or futile ones. However, those points will still occupy time in your opponent's submissions. If your opponent has simply been put to their proof they will still need to deal with the point sufficiently to convince the moot masters, whereas if a point is admitted they need not address it at all. Be aware though that there will be occasions where it is appropriate to admit an issue, particularly in professional practice. In each case it will be a matter of judgment.

## Address weaknesses in your case

Rarely, if ever, will an advocate have a case completely devoid of weaknesses. It is very unlikely to happen in a moot problem. If you believe your case is impenetrable, you are almost certainly missing something fundamental and run the risk of being taken by surprise in the actual moot.

Do not be afraid to deal with weaknesses in your case. Indeed doing so is likely to advance your position. Acknowledging a difficulty with your argument can have a number of consequences. First, you can lessen the impact of your opponent's submission. By identifying and quietly discussing the issue, you can downplay the significance of any weakness.

> Your Excellencies, this point is contentious. The Applicant acknowledges that first impressions may not be favourable to its case. There are authorities that do not support the interpretation submitted by the Applicant. The Respondent will undoubtedly refer this Honourable Court to many of those authorities and in particular the case of *Southmark* v *Deacon Hills* 222 VLR 45. But the Applicant strongly urges the Court not to be drawn into an overly simplistic analogy with that case. Every case must be determined on its own merits. The circumstances of the present case are different – so different in fact as to warrant a different conclusion. The differences are . . .

The physical delivery of a submission of this kind is critical. Do not be strident and forceful; be demure and calm. Identify the authorities that appear to be against you. Acknowledge that there is a certain appeal to the opposing argument, but dismiss it by implication. In the above example, the analogy is described as "overly simplistic". The demure and calm presentation will suggest a considered approach. The audience will appreciate that you have recognised and investigated the point, and are not overly concerned by it. In contrast, a strident and forceful submission will suggest that you are defensive about the point. Displaying defensiveness will create the impression that you are worried, and if you are worried your moot masters will be too.

## Handling questions

Although the prospect of dealing with questions may seem daunting, developing an ability to handle questions properly will distinguish you from other competitors in the moot. Well-answered questions can win both moots and real cases. Dialogue with your moot masters will allow you to identify the issues that are troubling them, and then to specifically address their concerns.

Preparing to answer questions is an integral part of structuring your oral argument. How can you predict the questions you are going to be asked? With a well-structured oral submission you will go beyond merely predicting questions to being in control of what is asked and when it is asked. Your ability to do this will be a product of your experience in many practice moots.

## Preparing for questions

When you first set about preparing your submission, you will probably have little or no idea about the questions you are likely to be asked. During a practice moot you will have an opportunity to test the effectiveness of your oral submission. Keep the time limits in mind, but do not worry if you exceed them during early stages of preparation. It is far better to run arguments and later remove them, than to never try them at all.

Every practice moot you do will tell you a little more about your submission. Take note of every question you are asked during a practice moot and subsequently analyse each question. Why was it asked? What was its purpose? How did you answer it? How should you have answered it?

This analysis will provide you with very important information about your oral submission – information that you should test by presenting your submission to as many different practice moot masters as you possibly can. It is this knowledge that will allow you to control the questions that are asked.

Over time you will find that some questions occur repeatedly at the same point in your submission. This suggests that whatever you are saying at that stage is prompting the question. Think about why it is being asked. Is it because the moot master has lost the flow of your argument? If so, then significant restructuring may be required. Is it because you have just contradicted an earlier submission? If so, then you may need to reorder your arguments. Is it because your argument is something new that intrigues the moot master? If so, then use the question as a springboard to show off your expertise in the subject matter. Do not underestimate the power of this knowledge.

## Incorporating questions into your structure

If you develop an appreciation for why a question is being asked, there are two ways of exploiting this knowledge. First, you can build the answer into your submission so that just as the question forms in the moot master's head you deliver the answer. This can leave a very positive impression because it demonstrates you have carefully thought through the issue. Alternatively, you can wait until the question is asked and use it to develop your submission or to show off your expertise. A word of warning, though – this can be tricky and can easily backfire if the question is not asked, or a different question is asked from the one you were expecting.

A common reason that questions are asked is because the moot master is seeking further explanation or clarification. Occasionally the moot master will rephrase the essence of your case as a question. This is only likely to happen in two situations. Perhaps you are presenting so well that the moot master is already making the conclusions you need. It can be a very satisfactory feeling if the moot master begins stating your case for you and suggests it is well structured. However, you are more likely to receive a question of this kind if the moot master wants to throw you a lifeline. You may have been floundering under a particular line of questions and the moot master wants to give you a way out. If so, you need to pay close attention to the question that is asked. If you did not hear it clearly, ask for it to be repeated.

Another common reason that moot masters ask questions is to test your knowledge. Some competitions give directions to the judges that questions should not be asked solely for this purpose, but it is almost inevitable that this will occur. Do not worry about this possibility, as you will be prepared to answer all of the questions of this kind. One indication that the question may be designed to test your knowledge is if it is a leading question. Leading questions are those where the answer is implicit in the actual question, and as such they generally only require a yes or no answer. If you are asked a leading question, it is possible that the moot master is trying to set a trap to expose what they see as a logical flaw in your submission. The challenge is to see the trap and avoid it. Again this will not be difficult if you have prepared thoroughly. You will begin to recognise lines of thinking and know how to respond. A particularly skilful answer will demonstrate not only that you can see what the moot master is doing, but that you have an answer to it as well.

> Yes, Your Excellency, that is correct. Is Your Excellency concerned that this position may be inconsistent with the Applicant's earlier submission that . . .

Another way that moot masters may seek to test your arguments is through the use of a hypothetical. Avoid these at all costs. While the moot itself is technically a hypothetical, it contains a lot of information. The hypotheticals you are likely to be asked during a moot by a moot master will be very general and will be constructed to conflict with your argument in some way. One way to avoid a hypothetical is to bring the moot master back to the main issues. It is possibly the only type of question you should dodge answering.

> The hypothetical Your Excellency suggests would certainly be a difficult one, and it is fortunate that this Honourable Court does not need to resolve it. What this Court must determine is whether on the facts available to it the Respondent wrongfully terminated the contract. The relevant question here is not if a valid notice had been sent, but was a valid notice sent. In the Applicant's submission it was not.

## Dealing with unpredicted questions

The structure of your submission will play an important role in assisting you to deal with unpredicted questions, particularly difficult ones.

Despite all this planning, there will be occasions when moot masters become fixated on a particular point and will simply not stop asking questions about it. You need to be conscious of the limited time you have available and the time taken up by these questions. There will be a stage at which it becomes more important to deliver the remainder of your submission rather than continuing to try to satisfy the moot master on the particular point. In other words, sometimes you have to "cut and run", and the structure of your submission will often dictate how effectively this can be done.

Knowing when and how to cut and run is something you will learn with practice. It is a judgment call you will need to make on the spot. By the time you reach the actual moot competition you will be acutely aware of how long your submission runs, and therefore have a good appreciation of how long you can spend discussing a particular point with the moot master. By this stage much of your thinking will occur subconsciously.

One factor that will play a part in your decision includes your assessment of how important the point is to your entire submission. This directly relates to the structure of the submission. Be prepared to abandon nearly every point you make. But if you abandon a point you need to have a backup reason why your client should win. You need an alternative argument.

Another factor that will influence your decision is the recognition that you should try to directly answer all questions put to you by the moot master. Always be prepared to make at least a reasonable attempt to satisfy the moot master. Responding to between two and four questions is a guide to what is reasonable. However, it cannot be stressed enough that you need to make a judgment call in each case. There is no hard and fast rule that applies to all situations. You will make the decision based on the unique situation that you find yourself in. Do not be daunted by this. Believe in your own ability and back it up with good preparation.

Give some thought to prepared phrases you can employ to effectively guillotine discussion on a point and move on. It is usually important to downplay the significance of the point in your overall submission. For instance, if it is one alternative of many, emphasise that fact and ask the moot master's permission to discuss one of the other alternatives instead.

> Your Honour, the point we have been discussing is only one alternative in the Applicant's case and I do not believe the submission can be made any differently. I am conscious of the time I have remaining, and with your permission I will turn to my next submission.

Where the argument does not have an alternative or is indeed the last of your alternatives, it is necessary to tell the moot master that you have nothing more to say. This should be done with some tact.

> Your Honour, this is the highest I can state my client's case and with your permission I will move on.

At this point it is pertinent to note the use of the first person in this example. Different forums (and indeed different moot masters) will have different conventions governing personal attribution in submissions, and it can be a matter of controversy. It is your client's case, but they are your submissions on behalf of your client. As a general rule, it is probably best to avoid presenting your submissions in the first person. What you personally think or believe is not relevant. Remember that you are representing a client's case, not your own. However, circumstances in which you need to cut and run may be an exception to that general rule. If you can cut short the moot master's questioning using the third person you should probably do so. But in essence you are making a personal plea to the moot master to let you get on with your submission, and so using the first person is often appropriate.

There may be some unpredicted questions that at first you do not know how to answer. Despite your thorough preparation and anticipation of possible questions, it would be foolhardy to think that there will never be such a question. You may well be asked a question you have never even contemplated before. A question like this can be particularly difficult to answer because you are unlikely to have done any preparatory work on that issue. In a real case you would normally ask permission to take the question on notice (that is, answer it later) and immediately research the issue. You do not have that luxury in a moot competition, and indeed it will not necessarily be afforded to you in real proceedings either. Rely on the techniques you employed when developing your structure to help you through.

The most important thing is not to panic. The second most important thing is not to look as though you are panicking. Pause, take a breath, and take a sip of water. While you are doing this, analyse the question in your mind in the same way you analysed questions during practice moots. Why was it asked? What did I say that prompted the question? Think about what stage you are at in your submission. This should provide a strong clue to the answer. Sometimes it is as simple as recognising that different people often ask essentially the same question in different ways. The number of questions you have analysed during preparation will probably have a direct correlation with your ability to analyse this difficult question on the spot. If the language of the moot is not your native tongue, this task may be additionally complicated. Do not be afraid to ask for the question to be restated. This has two benefits. First, you may recognise the restated question as one you already know the answer to, and second, it gives you more time. If after the question has been restated a second time you are still no closer to understanding the question, engage with the moot master and try to draw them into providing an explanation of their question.

> I apologise, Your Honour. So that I may respond directly to your concern, could you elaborate further?

As always, the method of delivery of questions like this will influence the response you receive. Be conscious not to imply by your manner that you think it is a silly question that does not make sense. Appear genuinely interested and concerned to answer the question properly. Positive body language can assist; gently nodding your head while the further explanation is being provided will give the impression you understand. The use of the first person is not controversial because you are not offering an opinion or belief.

Hopefully, by this stage you will now understand the question or at least be sufficiently confident to respond. In the event you still have absolutely no idea what you are being asked, bluff and fall back onto your structure. It is very important that you never lie or make up an authority you think will get you out of the situation. To do so would be unethical and is undoubtedly against the spirit of the moot. Furthermore, it is very unlikely to advance your situation in any way. There is a high probability that you will be exposed, either by the moot master or by your opponent. It is far better to move around the question. Politely dismiss the moot master's concern as not necessary in your client's submission, restate the signposts relevant to that stage, and then make it clear that you are moving on.

> (*After nodding gently*) Yes, Your Honour, in the Applicant's submission it is not necessary for this Honourable Court to be concerned with that point. Nothing would turn on it. Irrespective of whether the Court accepted or rejected any submissions the Applicant might make on the point, the Applicant's fundamental case would still stand. To establish liability the Respondent would need to demonstrate that there was a duty of care, and that it was breached. And in the Applicant's submission the Respondent cannot meet that burden.
>
> With your permission I will turn to the Applicant's alternative submission that . . .

If the moot master tries to keep you on the point you should make use of your "cut and run" phrase (see page 65). When doing so it may be wise to mention a concern about the remaining time.

## Getting help from your team-mates

Remember that advocacy is more often than not a team activity. In a moot there is usually at least one other person up there with you and frequently more. The same is true in professional practice. Your co-counsel may well know the answer to the question you are struggling to understand. Provided it is permitted under the rules of the competition, do not be afraid to utilise your collective knowledge. There are professional and amateurish ways of doing this.

If faced with a question you do not know the answer to, it is perfectly acceptable to ask for a moment to confer with your co-counsel. But doing so immediately creates an impression that you do not know the answer, or more detrimentally that you cannot answer. Instead develop signals you can send to your co-counsel that you need help. These signals should be completely invisible to the audience. One way is to assign particular meaning to phrases you would use generally in the course of your answer. For example, it might be agreed that if you say, "I am sorry, Your Honour, could you please repeat the question?" you think you know the answer and are just buying some time to formulate the reply. Whereas if you say, "I am sorry, Your Honour, could you please restate the question?" this could be a signal to your colleague that you have no idea. All that has changed is one word. To the audience it would mean nothing, but to your team members who know the signal it will mean a lot.

How your colleagues come to your assistance will vary. They may not know the answer either, in which case you will have to implement the procedure to overcome unanswerable questions outlined above. If your colleagues do know the answer, they may be able to quickly slide a note to you with the answer on it, or identify a passage you should cite from an authority. Alternatively, they may answer the question. In a number of competitions this will be allowed, but again there is a good and a bad way of doing it. Co-counsel should not simply jump in; rather you should refer the moot master to them.

> Your Honour, that is something my co-counsel has considered in detail, and with your indulgence I ask that she be allowed to respond to the question.

Be careful when utilising co-counsel in this way. It should be done sparingly, particularly if each advocate (as opposed to the team as a whole) is being graded by the moot master. Indeed, the rules of some competitions, such as Jessup, may preclude you from having any discussions with co-counsel, or passing notes.

## Varying the order in your submission

A good structure to your oral submission will allow you, the advocate, to easily jump to different points in the submission and address them out of order if necessary. Naturally, changing the order of your arguments in the middle of your submission is not likely to be a decision you have voluntarily made. Rather it will have been forced upon you by questions from the moot master.

There are two situations in which you encounter questions that do not coincide with where you are in your submission. In the first situation you are taken backwards, and the second takes you forwards in your submission.

Be ready for a moot master who allows you to complete your entire submission and then asks a question about the first or second point you made.

Alternatively, if a moot master asks you a question that relates to a matter further on in your submission go to it immediately. Never provide answers such as "I'm coming to that" or "I will be addressing that shortly". While it is not a cardinal sin, it is generally frowned upon both in moots and in real practice. The question will identify an issue that is of particular concern to the moot master. Part of your role as an advocate is to allay any concerns the moot master may have, therefore it is best to address the question immediately.

# RESPONDING TO A SUBMISSION

Although a moot is not a debate, it is very important that you respond to the submissions made by your opponent. This is often a variable that you will have little ability to anticipate, so you need to prepare for and make use of those areas that are in within your control.

One such area is the flexibility of your submission. The relative importance of different arguments within your submission will be affected by the submissions made by your opponent. For example, if your opponent concedes a particular issue it is not necessary for you to make significant submissions on it. This may give you an opportunity to include another argument that you had previously discarded because of time constraints. You cannot know this will happen until it actually occurs in the moot, and so you need to be able to adjust your structure at a moment's notice.

A much more difficult situation occurs when your opponent focuses on a point you had previously thought to be weak. This should not represent a substantive or content-based problem because your preparation will ensure that you are familiar with the point. However, it will impact on the structure of your submission. The emphasis of your submission must change. Be ready to pick up alternative arguments that you had previously discarded, and be prepared to drop other arguments that you wanted to make.

So, particularly in the context of responding, the architecture of your submission must be sound. You then simply add or remove content as appropriate. What content you should add or remove is principally governed by the submissions made by your opponents. It is very important, therefore, that you pay close attention while those submissions are being made.

You must also listen carefully and closely to the questions the moot master is asking your opponents. We have already discussed how questions tended to identify concerns or logical flaws in a submission. Whereas during the preparation stage you analysed these questions to improve your own case, now analyse them to help you critique the submissions made by your opponent. This can be done in two complementary ways. First, the substance of the questions to your opponents will suggest areas worthy of emphasis in your submission. Second, you can take the opportunity to involve the moot masters by referring back to their questions during your submission. When doing this, be careful not to imply that the moot master was actually making a point. Do not use expressions such as, "Your Honour was correct to question…" or "Your Honour made the point…". Moot masters may react negatively to phrases such as this, because they are not allowed to make a point at this stage of the moot. You are in effect implying that the moot masters have prejudged the merits of the case, albeit in your favour. Instead repeat the question, note its importance to your client, and respond.

During opposing counsel's submission, Madame President asked the question . . . We respectfully submit that this question does draw attention to what the Respondent says is a fatal flaw in the Applicant's case. In answering Madame President's question the Counsel for the Applicant suggested . . . The evidence simply cannot sustain such an argument.

Short passages like this are very easy to incorporate into a well-structured argument, because they do not change the underlying architecture of the submission at all. Responding in this way will earn the respect of the moot masters because it demonstrates that you know your case, you were listening to the opposition, and you are keen to engage with the moot masters on matters that are important to them.

# PRESENTING AN ORAL SUBMISSION

Not surprisingly there are considerable similarities between the advice offered for presentation of oral submissions and the advice offered for composing written documents. One very important common piece of advice is the value of developing an awareness of your environment. Just as different competitions call for different styles of written document, there will be stylistic differences in the oral presentation. For example, in courts you are expected to stand, whereas in arbitrations you would normally sit. In a court you refer to the judges with phrases such as "Your Honour" and "Your Worship", whereas in an arbitration you might address "Madam Arbitrator".

The peculiarities of each competition should be investigated very early in your preparation. You do not want to get into the habit of referring to your moot master in an incorrect manner. This book cannot list the stylistic requirements of every competition – there are simply too many differences in too many competitions. The task will be easy for you because you can research the requirements of the particular competition you are participating in!

Instead, we will be focusing on presentation issues that will be relevant to any form of oral advocacy. Indeed, much of the advice provided will be relevant to public speaking of any kind.

We have already discussed the importance of meeting audience expectations in the context of argument selection, but it is equally relevant to presentation. From the very moment you arrive at a moot, the moot master will have expectations as to how you should conduct yourself. Those expectations can probably be summed up in one word: "professional". To ensure that you appear as professional as possible, think about what it means to be professional in all aspects of your moot appearance. Many of the topics discussed below have an impact on how professional you appear.

## Preparation

We have discussed the importance of preparation many times. Whether you are competing in a prestigious international moot competition, or a small moot competition run by your law students' society, you should always be prepared to the best of your ability. Moot masters, whoever they may be, will always be influenced by how important the moot competition is to you. If you turn up unprepared it suggests you are not really concerned with the outcome, and this will reflect unfavourably upon you in any moot master's eyes.

## Physical appearance

How you dress can affect your presentation and the impression you leave upon the audience. Although in some parts of the world we are starting to see a relaxation in dress codes, there is still an almost universal presumption that professionals will wear suits. Furthermore, what might be acceptable in some cultures may not be acceptable in others.

It is always better to err on the side of caution and adopt the more conservative approach. By way of demonstration, consider the following events that occurred in a real moot. It was an unseasonably warm day, and as the moot was being conducted during a university break, the pre-programmed air-conditioning was not working. Because the door was closed, the room became stuffy and quite uncomfortable for everyone inside it, particularly the advocates. There were three moot masters: two from civil law jurisdictions and one from a common law jurisdiction. The common law moot master invited the advocates to take off their suit jackets. One team did; the other did not. The team that had taken off their jackets became increasingly dishevelled over the course of the moot: ties were loosened slightly, top buttons were undone, shirts revealed dark patches of sweat. They looked as though they were really struggling. In contrast, the team that kept their jackets on maintained a very professional image, notwithstanding the fact that they too were really struggling. At the end of the moot, the contrast in physical appearance between the two teams was so extraordinary that one of the civil law moot masters was moved to comment on it. After explaining that it would not affect his scoring on this occasion, the moot master went on to say that in his view removing suit jackets was tactically wrong and even disrespectful, notwithstanding the invitation from one of the moot masters to do so.

How you dress can also have a more subtle effect on your performance. Do not underestimate the influence of your dress on your psychological approach to the moot. We naturally distinguish the importance of an occasion by the clothes we wear. Just as other people will draw conclusions from your appearance, so will you. If you have gone to the trouble of having a haircut, wearing a nicely ironed shirt, putting on make-up or doing whatever it is you do to look good, you will feel good as well. If you feel good you will be confident, and confidence is a very appealing attribute.

# Time keeping

One of the strongest indications that advocates are in control is when they are acutely aware of the time their submission is taking. Time keeping is essential.

If the rules permit, this may be done by your co-counsel. For example, you may have a small piece of paper with various time intervals noted on it. When you only have 10 minutes left your co-counsel very quietly and inconspicuously crosses off the number 10. It is necessary to emphasise that this should be done without attracting any attention; kicking your colleague under the table is not advisable!

In competitions where counsel are not permitted to communicate with each other during a submission, the task is a little harder because you will need to do it yourself. In these circumstances it is important you have your own timing device; do not assume there will be a clock visible somewhere in the moot court. Be careful though that your timing device is not going to make any noise. For example, a countdown timer sounding at the end of 20 minutes is going to look very unprofessional, and will draw the attention of your moot masters to the fact that you are out of time.

Time keeping is a virtue that can lead to a vice: people often start to speak more quickly when they think they are running short of time. Resist this temptation. Instead, if necessary, make time in your submission by dropping one or two of your weaker alternative arguments. All of this can be pre-planned.

If you have 20 minutes in which to make your submission and you are expecting questions, do not plan to deliver a 20-minute submission. From your practice moots you will have a reasonable idea of how much time questions occupy. It is probably reasonable to assume that uninterrupted your submission would only last between 11 and 13 minutes. This is not very long, and therefore argument selection is very important. It is also another reason why there needs to be flexibility in the structure of your submission. Just as you may need to discard an alternative argument, you may wish to add one if you find that time is available. Well before you even enter the moot court, you should have decided that if you have not reached a particular point in your submission by the 10-minute mark, you will drop alternative C, for example. Preparing for situations like this will ensure that you remain in control. You are less likely to rush or to become overly stressed or worried, all of which would be reflected outwardly in your presentation. Rather, you will know what to do for every eventuality and how to do it.

## Opening formalities

The opening formalities begin with the announcement of your appearance, and encompass everything you do (or should do) from the moment the moot officially begins to the point when you actually begin your submission.

The very first formality you should be aware of is whether you should stand when the moot master enters the room. This may well depend on the type of moot you are participating in, and you should find out in advance what is required for your particular moot. However, as a general rule it is always polite to stand when you are being introduced to someone. It demonstrates respect.

Following the arrival of the moot master, there will usually be a request for appearances. The procedure for this may also differ depending on the forum. Some forums will have appearance slips that advocates will complete prior to the arrival of the moot master. In these competitions the moot master may well refer to each advocate by name and ask them to confirm that they appear for a particular side. On other occasions you will be expected to verbally announce your appearance. There will be particular customs you should adopt, depending on the forum.

> May it please the Court, my name is Smith, initial J, and I appear for the Applicant in this matter.

Alternatively it might be appropriate to say:

> Thank you, Mr President. My name is John Smith and I appear on behalf of the Applicant.

You will need to research what is appropriate for your particular competition.

You need to know who will be announcing appearances. If there are two of you, does the first speaker introduce both, or do you take turns? It may be a personal decision rather than one that needs to comply with any particular custom. Either way, make sure you and your partner know what is going to happen. You will not make a good start if you and another team member inadvertently speak at the same time.

There are several arguments in favour of each speaker introducing themselves. First, there will not be any concern about mispronouncing a name; and second it cannot be seen as being politically incorrect. The latter of these concerns rarely surfaces, but it is better to avoid even the slim possibility. Somewhat surprisingly it is not uncommon to see counsel stumble over the pronunciation of a colleague's name.

All appearances should be announced at the beginning of the moot. This is important in a real dispute because it serves to identify the advocates appearing. In the absence of an announcement, anyone might be sitting at the Bar table. Moot masters need to know who is who, and in what order they will be appearing. In competitions where moot masters allocate scores to individuals, identifying each person is a necessity. To assist in this identification process (and in the absence of appearance slips) some advocates will present the moot master with business cards, or have small name plates at the front of their desk. These can certainly be of great benefit to the moot master, but you need to decide whether they are appropriate for your competition.

Following appearances, the first speaker will normally address the moot master. Irrespective of who the first speaker is, it is usually appropriate to ask the moot masters whether they would like a brief summary of the facts. In the event this offer is accepted, you should have prepared a very concise and non-biased summary. This is not the time to use emotive language or to denigrate your opponent's case. Simply state the important facts leading up to the dispute and identify the issues for determination. Be aware that the statement of facts will be consuming your submission time so make sure you are brief.

The final opening formality you may or may not address before your submission is to ask whether full citations are required. Some advocates prefer to give the first full citation and then ask if they may be subsequently dispensed with. There is no ideal way of doing this, and the approach you choose will vary according to your impressions of the moot masters. It is important though, if you are the opposition counsel, not to assume the same courtesy will be automatically extended. You should clarify at the beginning of your submission whether the citations are required. Citations are often not required when they appear elsewhere, for example, in your written submissions. If this is the first reference ever, you should always offer the full citation. Most moot masters will accede to a request to dispense with citations because they appreciate that it is simply time-consuming in the context of a moot. Asking the question always indicates to the moot master that you are prepared to provide the citation if required. This is probably not a situation in which you want to call the moot master's bluff as it may reflect very poorly on your preparation.

# Using case materials

Your familiarity with the facts and materials of the case, and the degree to which you utilise them, will provide a strong indication of your control of your oral submission.

The facts of the problem play a very significant role in your submission. The first thing most audiences want to know is what happened. There is a certain logic to this. It would seem odd to look at the consequences of an action without first identifying the action itself. This means that you should state any relevant facts first, then the law, then the consequences of applying the law to the facts. It should be a familiar sequence to you as it is a frequently recommended method employed in legal exams.

To be able to do this well you need to develop an instantaneous recollection of the facts of the problem. Some people have what is commonly called a photographic memory. For those lucky few, remembering small details comes quickly and easily. If you are not one of those people, there are techniques you can employ to improve your abilities.

## Employing flash cards

One of the simplest ways to become familiar with case materials is to use flash cards. Flash cards are small palm-sized cards that have information on both sides. They can be used as a learning aid for many different tasks, such as learning foreign languages and mathematical tables.

In preparing for a moot, you might put a date on one side of a flash card and then anything significant about that date on the reverse side. Once you have a complete set of dates you can ask anyone to test your knowledge. This will probably be a team member but it could just as easily be a friend or family member. Indeed it is not even necessary to have someone else test you; you can do it yourself. If a friend is willing to help, have your friend randomly pick up a card and say the date. You need to list everything significant about that date as quickly as possible. The exercise can be reversed as well. Your friend says a significant event and you need to state the date. The more often you work with the flash cards the quicker you will become. Eventually you will reach the stage where the response instantly comes to you.

With a couple of minor additions, you can use these flash cards to improve your familiarity with the case materials as well. Include information such as page references, exhibit numbers or clarifications numbers. The effort you put into familiarising yourself carefully with the material will be justified the moment the moot master asks you, "And where do we find that?" Imagine how impressive it will look and how good you will feel if you can respond without pausing or breaking eye contact, "That is on page 6 of the Compromis, Your Honour." An intimate knowledge of the facts and materials also allows you to spot and politely expose any inaccuracies in your opponent's case. Learning the case this closely may take some time but it is well worth the effort.

## Using a casebook

Case materials encompass not only the official documentation provided by the competition, but any documentation used in the moot. Any written documentation you have supplied, such as an outline of submissions or casebook, is part of the case materials. It is very important that you also familiarise yourself with these documents and practise working with them effectively. The most significant of these is the casebook.

A casebook, as we have already noted, is a collection of all of the cases and authorities you intend to rely upon in your submissions. Frequently it will be necessary and appropriate to refer the moot masters to a particular passage in a judgment, or to particular remarks made by a legal commentator. When you do this, have the exact reference ready to offer the moot master. Make it very easy for the moot master to find what you are looking at. Once you have identified the reference, wait a moment and make sure that the moot master has found the spot before proceeding with your submission. There is no need to wait until you receive an indication from the moot master to proceed, although this will usually be forthcoming as soon as the master has found the appropriate passage. It is sufficient to pause for a few seconds and then keep going. Keep watching the moot master as you are speaking to ascertain whether the master is in fact listening to your submission or is fidgeting with the materials. If that appears to be the case, it is not inappropriate to ask whether the moot master has found the passage.

If you are competing in a moot competition that does not require a casebook, do not assume that this advice is irrelevant to you. Simply because you are not providing a copy of the actual material in the moot does not mean that you should not give specific references. Whenever you cite any authority, have a page or paragraph reference at the ready. It is less likely that you need to include this as part of your submission, but if asked by the moot master for the reference, you need to have it.

## Using materials appropriately

The final issue regarding case materials is how to use them appropriately. It is not necessary to refer to the materials every time you state a fact or make a point. The purpose of authority is to buttress your submission, and to highlight the relevance of what you are saying. When you do quote a passage from a case, a statute or commentary, make sure that you are not quoting it out of context. For example, an article in a convention may have multiple sub-articles, and you might be tempted to only read the sub-article that appears to support your case. That sub-article considered on its own might leave a very different impression than it would if discussed in its wider context. Moot masters are likely to notice this, and if they do not, you can be almost certain your opposition will. Once discovered, this will reflect badly on your submissions, as at one level it suggests an intention to mislead the moot master. It is perfectly acceptable for you to draw the moot master's attention to an important phrase or sub-article, but do this through emphasis. Use your voice to emphasise a passage, but keep the correct context.

# Voice and delivery

Your voice is one of the most extraordinary and powerful tools at your disposal. All of our voices are different. Some are naturally melodic and calming, others demand attention, a few have an undefinable yet distinct quality, and some are a bit thin or scratchy. Irrespective of how your voice might be described, we all have an ability to use our voices. You can be demure or forceful, inquisitive or authoritative, caring or dispassionate. You can convey all this simply by saying the same words in different ways. It would be a terrible shame to waste this tool – but waste it many do.

Often those judging your practice moots will be able to tell you whether or not you are taking full advantage of your voice. However, you can work on this by yourself as well. Get a recording device and record yourself. If you have never heard a recording of yourself before, be prepared for a shock. Your voice will sound very different, possibly even unrecognisable! When you listen to a recording of yourself you are hearing your voice the way everyone else does. The physiological reasons why we hear ourselves differently are not important, but it is worthwhile being aware of the phenomenon.

## Moderate your tone, pitch and accent

Once you have recovered from the shock, listen critically to your performance. In particular, focus on your intonation – the tone and pitch of your voice. Speaking in a monotone should be avoided. Even though the subject matter may be extremely interesting, if the presentation is delivered in a monotonous fashion it will almost invariably be labelled by the audience as boring. Make sure you vary your tone appropriately throughout your submission.

It is possible to vary tone inappropriately, and this will simply serve to confuse your audience. Your audience needs to understand the significance of the various tones you adopt. To be able to do this, there needs to be a consistency in your use of tone, and each change must have a particular implication. There are common conventions about what changes of tone mean in every language; they are not arbitrarily decided upon by an individual speaker. For example, in English we naturally tend to finish questions on a higher pitch.

Different languages use pitch and tones in different ways. This is evident simply from the fact that we have different accents. Accents are an important consideration, particularly for native speakers of the language. The fact that you can speak English perfectly will be of little value if your accent prevents you from being understood. Ideally you should aim to have your accent sound as neutral as possible. This can, in part, be achieved by simply making sure you enunciate every word and round your vowels.

The issue of accents is not something that should alarm or concern non-native speakers. Indeed we should have nothing but support, praise and admiration for participants who can moot in a second language. However, to completely ignore the fact that there will be some language difficulties for non-native speakers would be silly. In most moot competitions, judges will be specifically instructed not to allow their scoring to be influenced by difficulties of this kind. The easiest way to avoid any kind of language difficulty is to keep your sentences short and simple. This is good advice that applies to everyone.

## Speak slowly

Concentrate on speaking slowly. It is almost impossible to speak too slowly. This will have two natural consequences. First, you will automatically begin to fully pronounce each word, which will help you speak clearly. Second, it will give your audience an opportunity to hear and comprehend each word. If you speak too quickly, your audience will hear a string of meaningless sounds. Learning to do this is not as easy as it may seem, and will require practice. You have to battle against the normal impulse to rush in circumstances where you have a lot to say and very little time to say it in.

## Moderate the volume

You should also be very conscious of whether you are speaking loudly or quietly. Just as people find it difficult to believe they are speaking too quickly, many people seem surprised by the suggestion that they naturally speak too softly. Your voice should fill the room to ensure that everyone, especially the moot masters, can hear you easily. Be careful not to yell, but err on the side of being slightly louder than you think you need to be, and this will ensure that your voice will carry to everyone in the room.

# Body language

The way you use your body as you deliver your submission can speak volumes to your audience. Often subconsciously our body language can reveal our true feelings. Sometimes we can control these reactions and on other occasions we cannot. For example, some people blush when they are nervous. Then when they sense that they are blushing they get even more nervous and embarrassed. The cure is to try to be less nervous and certainly not be embarrassed if you start to blush. Admittedly, this is much easier said than done, but it is true that solid preparation and earned self-confidence do wonders to combat nervousness.

## Never fidget

Nervousness can cause some people to fidget during their presentations, for example, clicking pens or tapping their fingers or feet. A habit of this kind has several disadvantages. It undermines the confident appearance you are trying to present, and it distracts the attention of your moot masters from what you are saying.

Precisely how you cure fidgeting will depend on your environment. If you are standing at a lectern you may be able to discreetly hold the lectern, to stop yourself tapping your fingers. If possible, this should not be seen by the moot master. Instead all the moot master should see is an advocate standing upright and paying attention to the task. Your hands are firmly holding the lectern so as to not reveal your state of anxiety. Alternatively, if you are sitting at a table, sit at the front of your seat, join your hands together and place them on the edge of the table. Concentrate on feeling the table just below the base of your little fingers. Sitting in this fashion allows you to push against the table as firmly as you like and it will not be noticed by the moot master. Furthermore, exerting pressure on that part of your hand will make it harder to wiggle your fingers.

## Make use of gestures and posture

Once you have mastered your body language sufficiently so that it will not detract from your submission, begin experimenting with ways of using it to your advantage. Hand movements can be very effective when adding emphasis, as can taking off glasses. Give some thought to how you use your body. What hand movements do you use subconsciously at the moment? How can you utilise them to improve your delivery? Get feedback from your coach and team members about your gestures. Your gestures should add emphasis to what you are saying and create a favourable impression. They should never be distracting or overdone.

Hands are only one part of our body though, and how we carry ourselves is also very important. You need to have good posture. Make sure you are standing upright and are not stooped over. If you are sitting down, do not relax back into the chair. Put both feet firmly on the ground and sit up straight. This is most easily achieved by sitting at the front of your chair.

## Pay attention

It stands to reason that if body language is a form of communication, then we are in fact communicating all the time. Just because you are not actually saying anything to the moot masters at a particular moment, you will still be conveying a message to them. The lesson here is that you must pay attention during the whole moot. Do not start looking out the window or back over your shoulder to the audience when your co-counsel is speaking. This can have a very negative impact on the impression created by your co-counsel's submission. If you do not think it is worth listening to, why should the moot master?

When the opposition are delivering their submission you must also pay attention. The message you send by not paying attention during your opponent's submission is not that the submission is not important, but rather that you are rude.

Maintaining a proper posture will in fact help you pay attention. This can be very important if a moot master turns around and asks you an unexpected question.

# Speaking from notes

The use of notes during a presentation is a hotly debated topic. Should you script your presentation and rote learn it? Should you have a complete copy in front of you when presenting, or should you just have a list of key points? The best advice is to do what suits you.

## Using a complete script

Many people will tell you not to script your presentation and certainly not to have it written word for word in front of you. This advice is misguided to the extent that it will force some people well outside their comfort zone, which will be detrimental to their overall performance. Remember, maintaining a relaxed, measured and confident approach is the most important goal. If having a complete script works for you then do it. The question then becomes how do you know if it is working?

The two most common criticisms of the use of scripts are that people tend to read and that they then lack flexibility. In a moot it is very important not to read. You need to be looking up at the moot masters and talking directly to them. It is virtually impossible to engage with someone if you are not looking at them. Reading also tends to impact on your tone. It is much easier to slip into a monotone if you are reading. It will also affect your volume. Our mouths point in the same direction as our eyes, therefore when reading out aloud we are quite literally speaking down to the paper, and not projecting our voices. In short, reading will detract from your submission and should be avoided as much as possible.

People who read will also tend to stick to their script. This affects their ability to answer questions. The need for flexibility was briefly discussed under the heading "Varying the order in your submission" (see page 69), and it is an equally relevant consideration at this stage. Moot masters will move you around your presentation, possibly at the most inconvenient stages. If you are relying on reading your submission, you will need to be able to sort through your notes instantaneously. This can be difficult for you and distracting for the moot master.

You need to establish what is right for you during your practice moots. Try different approaches and see how they work. Think about the environment you will be in when delivering your submission. If you are sitting or standing at a chest-high lectern, the actual act of turning a page will occur very close to your face and certainly within the field of vision of the moot master. Any movement like this can be distracting, particularly if it is accompanied by the creaking of an exercise book. Instead, you could try using sheets of paper that are not bound, as they can be slid from one side of the lectern to the other in a very subtle movement. The danger is, of course, that your pages may end up in the wrong order, therefore it is important to use clearly visible page numbers. It would also be sensible to check that all your pages are present and in the right order just before beginning your presentation.

For those of you who feel most comfortable with a complete script in front of you, develop techniques that will minimise the negative impression that can be created by reading. You need to be able to move very easily between your notes and the moot master. As a consequence, you cannot be wasting time trying to find the passage you were up to on the page just before you looked away. Keep your pages clear and uncluttered. Make sure your submission is printed in a large, easy-to-read font with a double space between each line. This document needs to be functional and versatile; it does not need to win design awards!

## Using summarised notes

If you decide that you are going to use notes, practise using them and think about how they should be designed for maximum effectiveness. For example, it may be advisable not to bind your notes in any way. This means you should not use an exercise book, or staple your notes together. This will allow you greater flexibility to vary the order of your presentation in response to questions from the moot master, as we have already discussed.

Notes can be a very effective and useful tool when used well. You need to give some thought to how your notes can best be designed to suit your requirements. It was suggested earlier that rather than speed up when you are running out of time it is far better to discard arguments. To be in a position to do this, you need to have prioritised your arguments. Which arguments are essential, which are desirable and which are dispensable, but would still be included in an ideal presentation? How you have designed your notes can greatly assist you in this process.

Divide a single sheet of paper into three columns. In the first column list all of the essential arguments. These are the arguments you believe you must present in your submission. In the second column list all the arguments that you consider would be desirable to include. Finally, in the last column list the less important arguments that you would still like to include in an ideal presentation. During your presentation, work your way through these lists. Be aware though that the priority of some arguments may change based on your opponent's submissions. As your opponents make the corresponding argument, tick it off your list. Now if you face any time pressures during your submission you will know which arguments you must raise, and which ones you can abandon.

When designing your notes, you need to consider whether you intend to write extra notes during the moot. If so, you will need to make sure there is room for you to do this in your notes, whether it is simply in the margin or in a designated place. Because you will be familiar with the arguments for both sides, you may have developed a list of common rebuttal points, and you may want to add to the list as the moot progresses if new arguments occur to you. If you do develop such a list, be sure to use it wisely and not inadvertently misuse the rebuttal procedure. Rebuttal is discussed in detail on pages 90–1.

## Using notes well

When using notes, whether it is a full script or dot points, the key is to know how to use those notes. Notes should never contain substantive issues to be researched on the spot. They are really only there as a security blanket, to reassure you. The same is true of open book law exams. You do not have the time to research in the middle of the exam, and neither do you in a moot. Never assume you will find the answer to a question in your notes. The notes may point you in the right direction, but the answer always comes from what you already know.

If the rules of your moot permit, you can also use notes to communicate with your team-mates. Typically these are used for time management or when responding, whether as an advocate for the party defending the claim or for the party bringing the claim in rebuttal.

## Building rapport with the moot master

People who are naturally charismatic and charming seem to effortlessly command attention when they walk into a room. They have vibrant personalities and can socialise easily. They have a presence, and always seem to impress an audience. These people can be extremely intimidating to those who do not see the same characteristics in themselves.

It is often the case that how we see ourselves is very different from the way others see us. Many of us tend to assume the worst. This is particularly true of people in stressful situations. Imagine you walk into a moot court and glance at the moot master. At that precise moment the moot master appears to sneer at you. What do you think? Do you assume you are already off to a bad start and basically give up without having said a word? The real reason for the moot master's apparent sneer might have nothing to do with you whatsoever. It may have been the onset of a sneeze, for instance.

The attractive and endearing people you may feel intimidated by are the ones who have learnt to overcome their negative assumptions about how others perceive them. These people are generally very comfortable with who they are, and their charisma comes from confidence and self-belief. Everyone can develop self-confidence, and you can too. Confidence in your abilities will be invaluable in helping you build a good rapport with the moot master.

To develop rapport with someone, you must engage with them. The tips on presentation that we have discussed so far play an important role in that engagement. Knowing that you are prepared will give you confidence. Your physical appearance, voice and body language will all show respect. Good time keeping demonstrates that you are in control of your presentation. Finally, and arguably most importantly, your use of the case materials and your notes will involve the moot master. You should aim to create a dialogue with the moot master, during which you maintain eye contract. Eye contact is important because it subconsciously suggests you are both honest and earnest.

An oral submission, like a job interview, is best when it is a dialogue. How that dialogue progresses will, to a large extent, depend on your attitude. Be yourself and let your own personality shine through your submission, just as you would in a job interview. Some people try to act their way through as if they were performers on a theatrical stage. Acting invariably involves pretending that you are someone you are not. It can be quite difficult to build rapport if you are acting. There is nothing to endear you to the moot master since by its very nature acting implies something false. When we watch actors on the stage or screen we suspend our disbelief because we already know and understand that it is a contrived scenario. There is no such understanding in a moot competition. It is certainly a contrived set of facts, but your performance should be a genuine one. If you are yourself and sincerely want to engage with the moot master, you will succeed. The shy and timid but very well prepared advocate will ultimately be much more engaging than a loud, brash, character actor.

## Multiple moot masters

Convincing one person can be relatively easy. If you have three moot masters, you may think that your task will be three times harder. This is not necessarily the case, although there is no doubt that it is harder to some degree. Fortunately, it is possible to overcome many of these difficulties with practice.

The most difficult aspect of appearing before multiple moot masters is establishing a rapport with all of them simultaneously. It is physically impossible to make eye contact with more than one person at a time, so you will need to divide your attention between each of the moot masters. This can be particularly difficult when one of the moot masters does not appear to be making any attempt to engage with you. For example, where only two of the three moot masters are asking questions, it is very easy to ignore the third. But you would do so at your peril. This moot master needs to receive an equal share of your attention because each moot master has the same capacity to award points and is therefore equally important to you.

If your competition has multiple moot masters, your practice moots should have the same number. Get used to shifting your attention between each moot master, especially those who do not seem to be paying attention. It is an unfortunate and unfair reality that the moot master who does not pay attention will be the one who complains that you have failed to engage them.

If you find that you are having some difficulty attracting the attention of a moot master simply by looking at them, there are a number of techniques you can use to politely demand their attention. First, as we have already discussed, you need to make the most of your voice and body language. If this is not enough, you can incorporate a direct reference to the moot master into your presentation by referring to them by their title or name.

Referring directly to a moot master must be done with care. The easiest method is to refer to a question that the moot master asked earlier in the moot. A more contentious method is to use information about the moot master that you know from outside the confines of the hearing that you are presently participating in. For example, you may know that the moot master comes from a civil or common law background. Or you may somehow draw upon a journal article or case decision that the particular moot master has written. If you are able to research your moot masters, you should do so. You may never use the information you find, but it is there in your arsenal if necessary.

The other information you should seek is the personal style of each of the moot masters. Are they the kind who will pester you with questions? Are they the kind who will want to hear more about the facts or the law? Are they likely to focus on one particular issue? Having all of this information will help you prepare for your presentation. At the very least it will give you an idea of what to expect, which is particularly important if you are appearing before a moot master with an aggressive style.

## Know how the moot is to be run

There are many procedural matters that you need to be familiar with so that there are no unpleasant surprises during the moot. Some of these may change from moot to moot, and even within the same competition, so it is important to practise for all eventualities. We have already discussed time keeping (see pages 73–4), but there are many other aspects to consider.

## Order of submissions

Advocates are frequently taken by surprise when the moot master changes the order of submissions. For example, the Respondent may have challenged the jurisdiction of the court. In this situation it would not be unreasonable if the Respondent was asked to make its submission on that issue first. Suddenly the Respondent is not responding any more but presenting an affirmative case. It is also important to remember that the first speaker should always offer a summary of the facts, and this means it may be the Respondent who has to present this summary.

## Rebuttal

The availability of rebuttal will vary from moot to moot. If you are representing the party bringing the case, always request a right of rebuttal. This is not to say you will always exercise that right, but have it up your sleeve if it is granted. If possible confer with your opposition before the moot begins and agree on how you would jointly like the moot to be run. The moot masters may ask whether there has been any agreement on these issues, or they may simply begin the moot. In either case the first advocate, whichever side the advocate represents, should clarify the procedure with the moot master – in particular the time available to each advocate, the order of arguments and the right of rebuttal (and occasionally sur-rebuttal). This can be done very politely by indicating that there were discussions between counsel before proceedings began and that you are jointly proposing a particular procedure to the moot master. The moot master may acquiesce or allow some matters like rebuttal. Ultimately it remains in the moot masters' hands and you can only ask.

Even if you have the right of rebuttal, you may not always wish to exercise it. Knowing when to rebut and when not to will come from an understanding of the purpose of rebuttal. Rebuttal does not exist so that you get the last chance to restate your case. On the contrary, rebuttal should not involve a restatement of the case at all. Rebuttal should be used sparingly and pointedly only to address new points raised by your opposition in the course of their submission. This is why it is particularly important for parties bringing a case to reserve the right.

Imagine you are the Applicant. Having run short of time you decided not to present one of your alternatives. During the Respondent's submission the alternative was raised with apparent acceptance by the moot master. This is when you use your rebuttal. But do not launch into your entire presentation on the point. Simply single out the fatal flaw without going further. It is the perfect example of when less is more. Sadly misuse and even abuse of the right of rebuttal has become the norm. The positive consequence though is that the proper use of rebuttal is striking and usually rewarded. When asked if you have any rebuttal, do not be afraid to say that you do not.

> No, the Applicant believes it has already answered all of the Respondent's submissions.

If you do have rebuttal, state the number of rebuttal points you will be making.

> Thank you, the Applicant has four points to make in rebuttal.

Limit yourself to the four, or at the very most five, strongest points. Doing so will suggest you appreciate that a rebuttal must be focused. You are likely to have five minutes at most, and at one issue per minute you may already be speaking too quickly.

There is one final point to make about rebuttal. Advocates who have not paid attention to their opponent's submission will not be able to rebut effectively. If after your submission you were completely preoccupied with what you were going to have for lunch, do not even try a rebuttal. You may have gleaned the general theme of your opponent's submission, but you will have no appreciation of the specificities, and it is the specificities that you should rebut on. So in addition to looking like you are paying attention, make sure that you actually do.

# Dealing with mistakes

Good preparation is preparation that prepares you for every contingency. However unlikely you may wish it to be, it is possible that you will make a mistake. In a moot, and often in real life, that fact that you have made a mistake is not as relevant as how you deal with it.

Sadly, ignoring a mistake will not make it go away. If you have made a mistake do not be frightened to correct it. It is far better to acknowledge that you "spoke in error" and to correct any misunderstanding that the moot master may have, than to simply push on. However, do not be too quick to assume that it is you who has indeed made an error, particularly if the moot master has suggested that one of your well-researched arguments is wrong. Remember that you will know much more about the problem than your moot master because of your extensive and detailed research on the topic. Have confidence in yourself and your submissions. Restate your proposition and clarify with the moot master precisely why they believe there is an error. If it is there, acknowledge it, downplay its significance to your overall submission and move on. If the moot master is wrong, take a moment to re-explain your point, specifically identifying why you are not in error and move on. When doing so you should not attribute the confusion to anyone.

> Your Worship, perhaps I could rephrase this point . . .

Irrespective of who is actually in error, the crucial point is to proceed with your submission. Battle on. Do not lose confidence or be too embarrassed to proceed. Standing dumbstruck, not knowing what to do next, will have a much greater impact on the moot master than merely acknowledging a mistake.

# CONTINUE THE TEAM WORK

The importance of teamwork has been repeatedly emphasised throughout this book. Although a team may only comprise two people, it is still a team.

Often you will find you most need your team-mates during your moot and immediately afterwards. If the rules permit, your team-mates can assist you when you are actually presenting. They can find references for you, pass you documents, keep time, and perhaps even assist with the answer to a question. All of these things have been canvassed in other sections of the book. However, something we have not yet discussed is how team-mates can assist after a presentation.

Watching a team-mate (or a student if you are the coach) presenting a submission can be extremely difficult. Because you have gone through the same or similar preparation, you will naturally think of answers to the questions being asked. Often you will think these answers are better than the ones your team-mate ultimately gives. You will be sitting in the audience thinking, "You know this . . . no, no, that's not right!" The problem is often exacerbated if there has been competition for the advocate's position. Irrespective of your personal feelings you must remember that you are part of a team, and you should only do what is right for the team. There is no certainty that if you had been speaking you would have answered the question any differently. The answer that pops into your head while sitting in the audience occurs to you in entirely different circumstances. You are not under the same pressure as your team-mate who is presenting and is the focus of everyone's attention. It is impossible to know how you would respond if you faced the same question under similar pressure and attention.

Accordingly, you should never criticise your team-mate's performance. Attacking your team-mates or denigrating their effort in any way, whether directly to them or to other team-mates, will only serve to lessen everyone's performance. Instead work with your team-mates in a positive fashion. Make sure that any feedback you have is constructive, and expressed in such a way that does not suggest fault. Confidence is king, and negative comments from team-mates can often be very damaging.

# Chapter 7

# Practice moots

The value of participating in practice moots cannot be under-estimated. The more familiar you become with the experience of standing before an audience presenting a submission, the more relaxed you will be when it comes to appearing in the moot competition. As we have discussed, relaxation, preparation and practice are the keys to performing at your best.

Elite athletes not only undergo intensive physical training, they often engage sports psychologists. A sports psychologist can help an athlete visualise various scenarios that might occur during a race, for example. By thinking through these scenarios, the athlete is prepared and will know what to do if any of the situations arise. While moot participants would rarely if ever call upon a psychologist, there are similarities in our preparation techniques. However, we have one considerable advantage over the athletes – we can actually experience the scenarios during practice moots, rather than just imagining them.

When establishing your program of practice moots, you should do so in a manner that exposes you to the greatest diversity of circumstances that might occur in the actual moot.

## WHEN TO START DOING PRACTICE MOOTS

You should begin practice moots as early as possible in the process of preparing for the competition. This is particularly important if you have little or no previous mooting experience. If you begin to articulate your arguments in the face of questioning, this will help you develop those arguments during the written stage as well. However, depending on the deadline for submission of the written document, and the time commitment required to produce it, opportunities to conduct practice moots may be limited. Once the document stage of the competition is completed, you should focus intensely on practice moots.

It is a sensible idea to allocate the responsibility for scheduling practice moots to one person within the team. This person will need to ensure that everyone participates in an equal number of practice moots. The same person should be responsible for coordinating moot masters. We discuss the different types of practice moot masters you should look for below; suffice to say you should aim for as many different ones as possible. As ideally you will have a large number of moot masters, one point of coordination is essential.

# WHO CAN BE A PRACTICE MOOT MASTER?

There are absolutely no qualifications necessary to be a practice moot master. This means that not only do practice moot masters not need to be experts in a particular area of law, they need not know anything about the law at all! There is no reason why parents and friends should not hear practice moots. You will, of course, need expert moot masters as well, but having moot masters with different skills and backgrounds can be extremely useful.

The purpose of practice moots is twofold. The more often you actually say your submission aloud, the more comfortable you will become. Secondly, practice moots should expose you to the different twists and turns that you may experience in the actual moot. The moot master will be the source of these twists and turns.

## Variety is key

Moot masters, along with your opponent's submission, are the principal and most unpredictable variable in a moot. Everything else about the moot is a constant. You know how long you will have to deliver your submission. You know the content of the problem. Because these aspects are completely predictable, they are very easy to incorporate into your preparation. Different moot masters will need to be handled in different ways, as you attempt to steer them towards asking the questions you wish them to ask. You learn this skill by experiencing as many different moot masters as possible.

Moot masters must be handled in different ways because they have different personalities. People will naturally react differently to particular submissions; some may not immediately grasp the argument, while others understand it instantly. Some moot masters will have prepared, and others will not have even read the first page of the materials. There will be those who are genuinely interested in your innovative approach, and others too beset by preconceived ideas to listen to an argument they had not previously considered. This is why you should engage as many different practice moot masters as possible.

However, do not worry if you only have a limited number of practice moot masters to call upon. Ask them to adopt different personas each time they moot. For example, sometimes they could be very interventionist, and on other occasions almost mute. During some moots they should concentrate on the substantive content of your submissions, and in other moots simply critique your presentation.

## Using experienced moot masters

Although anyone can be a moot master, there are moot masters with particular experience that will be most helpful to you: previous participants of the competition; students with experience of other moots; your lecturers; and eminent and professionally intimidating legal practitioners.

Previous participants, the alumni of the competition, are particularly valuable as moot masters because they have direct experience of your competition environment. They will be able to replicate the conduct of real competition moot masters. They are also likely to have been through a similar training process to the one you are currently embarking upon. Although the currency of their knowledge of the subject matter may wane over time, their critique of your substantive arguments will be invaluable. Similarly they will be able to provide advice on your presentation skills.

Students who have experience of other moots and your lecturers will be able to provide you with criticism of the logical coherence of your substantive arguments and general advice on presentation.

Professionally intimidating legal practitioners can add an extra dimension to your practice moot preparation. Typically, they will be renowned experts in the relevant field of law, such as judges or eminent academics. Many of these people will be more than happy to hear a practice moot for you. But it is likely to be only one moot, so you should schedule the moot when it will be of most benefit. To ensure that you are not wasting their time or yours, it is best to schedule moots with these moot masters in the final stages of your preparation. Moot masters of this kind will be most like the real moot masters that you will encounter at the competition, as they will generally come from the same echelon of the legal profession. In the competition itself, you will be appearing before very senior judges and other prominent and leading members of the international legal community. As a consequence, these particular practice moots can be very valuable. Because of the eminence of the moot master, these practice moots take on a greater importance. This means you will experience more tension, more apprehension and a heightened state of nervousness – all the things you will need to deal with in the actual competition. It is often in these moots that you will begin to learn how to deal with any fear you may have.

## MAKING THE MOST OF PRACTICE MOOTS

Simply doing a practice moot will benefit any participant. It is how you utilise the practice moot experience that will distinguish your preparation from others in the competition. Earlier in the book we discussed the benefits associated with noting and analysing the questions you are asked during these moots (see pages 61–2). Because it is so important, it is worthwhile repeating here.

Make a list of all the questions you have been asked during your practice moots. As a team, compile a group list and then discuss the best answer to each question. Remember that appropriate answers may vary depending on the context in which the question is asked, but the basis of the answer will probably always be the same. In this way the team as a whole will get the benefit of collective knowledge and experience. Everyone in your team should be regularly reading this list and using it to improve their individual submissions.

## Record the moot

If you have the resources available, it is a good idea to record your practice moots. A video recording is a very useful tool for a post-moot analysis. If everyone is aware the moot is being recorded, it will curb their inclination to interrupt the moot to offer comment or criticism. Afterwards you can simply review the videotape, pause it appropriately and discuss how a particular question was answered.

When you are preparing to videotape a moot, you should ideally position the camera in such a way that you can see all advocates at once. This will allow people to review their body language when they are not actively participating. It can be surprising how often advocates are certain that they were paying attention throughout the moot, but the video footage suggests otherwise.

# INTER-VARSITY PRACTICE MOOTS

In some competitions there may be an opportunity to conduct practice moots with other university teams before the competition itself. Sometimes referred to as "pre-moots", these are often amongst the most valuable practice moots your team will do if they are conducted in the right manner.

A pre-moot provides an opportunity for you to test yourself against an unfamiliar opposition. Mooting against your own team-mates occurs in a false environment, because you are already intimately acquainted not only with their arguments but with how they will run those arguments. As a consequence, your response, even if you are genuinely responding, will always have an element of pre-meditation. In a pre-moot, you will be familiar with most of the arguments that will be raised by your opposition, but how they are actually presented will be unpredictable. Thus it is an opportunity to really work on your ability to respond.

Pre-moots inevitably raise concerns that you will be revealing your arguments to your opposition in advance of the competition itself. While this is an understandable concern, it is not one of any real consequence. You should never conduct a pre-moot against a team you know with certainty you will be facing in the competition. However, you may well find that you do meet some of your pre-moot partners in the finals. This may at first seem a little unfortunate but may not be avoidable. There are two principal reasons why it should not be of great concern. First, it is very unlikely another team will be able to implement, overnight, an argument you have been developing for months. Second, if you have followed the advice given earlier in this book, you will already have an argument that overcomes that point.

Despite this advice, participants will undoubtedly still struggle with the decision about whether or not to run all their arguments. The best place to seek an answer to that question is with the moot master. If the moot master is someone whom you know will be subsequently judging in the actual competition, it is probably a sound idea to run any of your more controversial arguments. Gauge the response: was it summarily dismissed or did it create interest? Forget that the other team is listening and make the most of your opportunity. If you happen to benefit another team, be proud that your argument was considered worthy. Make no mistake, it will be painful if you see a team you met in a pre-moot using your arguments in a final, but the benefits of these moots do generally outweigh that risk.

# Chapter 8

# The competition itself

## GETTING THERE

The logistics involved in getting your team to the moot competition can be surprisingly complex, so you must begin to plan very early in the process. You need to organise transport, accommodation, current passports and visas.

Most teams will be operating on a fairly tight budget. It is sensible to book flights and accommodation as early as possible because this is usually when the cheapest fares are available. This will help avoid unnecessary stress and complications as you approach the crucial oral stages of the competition.

Just as you may have appointed one person to be responsible for fundraising, it may be appropriate to appoint one person to be responsible for coordinating all your travel and accommodation requirements. This is not an easy job. Frequently participants decide to take the opportunity for holidays or sightseeing, and thus have divergent travel plans. The person arranging transport and accommodation for the whole team will need to coordinate multiple itineraries.

This may be your first trip overseas, and this will be the case for many participants in international moot competitions. Or, if you have been overseas before, it may have been on a family holiday. Travelling overseas for the first time can be a daunting but very rewarding experience. Given that you are doing this in the context of a competition, fears may be multiplied. There is no need to be fearful or concerned. You will be travelling with a group of people whom you have probably spent the last few months virtually living with. As a team you should be supportive and look after each other through this process.

One of the greatest concerns people have when travelling is the fear of getting lost. This is not an irrational fear, particularly if you are going somewhere where you cannot speak the language. However, it is something you can prepare for. Each member of the team should ensure that they personally know all the travel and accommodation information. This is not something to be delegated, as in the event that you do become separated from your team you need to know what to do.

If possible, familiarise yourself with your intended destination before you actually depart. You can do this by looking at a map and ascertaining the general location of major landmarks, including the location of the competition, in relation to your accommodation. Good travelling maps can be bought very easily from bookstores, or you can view maps on the internet. Moot participants frequently return with stories of missed connections, lost luggage and even lost team-mates. It is something you will laugh about later, but at the time it can be emotionally testing.

If possible, try to arrive in the city where the moot is to be held a day or two early. This will allow you to relax in your new environment. Establish how you plan to move from your accommodation to the moot venue. How long will it take? Actually try it out and make sure you know where you are going. Apart from simply being a fun act of exploring, testing your intended route also serves a very important purpose in your preparation for the competition. We know that a competition moot is a highly stressful environment, but we also know that those who can remain calm and relaxed have a greater chance of doing well. It stands to reason that you should eliminate any additional and unnecessary sources of stress and anxiety wherever possible. The fear of getting lost on the way to the moot, or even just of being late, is very easily avoided by travelling the route beforehand.

There are many other fears and questions that will arise when travelling. Many of them you may not even appreciate until they actually descend upon you. For example, when you first pull your suit out of your suitcase it will inevitably be crushed. What do you do? You are not sure whether you can iron it, and the hotel dry-cleaning service is extremely expensive. An experienced traveller will tell you that to remove most of these creases simply hang your suit in the bathroom of your hotel or any environment with steam. You are effectively going to steam your suit. The creases will naturally fall out.

Speak to people who have travelled to your destination before, and get as many travel tips as you can. Ask them about whether it is better for you to carry cash or credit cards. Should you get cash before you leave or when you arrive? Should you carry your passport on you at all times? Discussing these issues well before you leave for the competition should remove any apprehension you may have about what to do.

# DURING THE COMPETITION

How you conduct yourself during the competition is very important. You are representing yourself, your university and possibly even your country, so it is important that you behave in an appropriate manner. This relates to both moot and non-moot activities.

Above all, make sure you are a good competitor and always act in accordance with the spirit of the competition. At an international moot, the spirit of the competition will always be one of bringing people together, friendship, learning and experience. Particularly to the competition organisers, these aspirations will be much more important than the act of competition. For participants it is easy to reverse these aspirations and be more concerned with winning than with the spirit of the competition.

This can lead to some difficult choices and not everyone will agree on the right choices to make. For example, some competitions permit you to watch other teams during the general rounds. Many participants will avail themselves of this opportunity but for a variety of reasons. Some will have made friends with the advocates and be there in support. Others will be interested in watching and learning from teams they anticipate will be very good. Either of these reasons is comfortably within the spirit of the competition. However, there will be some participants who deliberately go to other moots with the intention of "stealing" arguments. Stealing is clearly not within the spirit of the competition. It is also not particularly smart as it is likely to have detrimental results.

Using stolen arguments is unintelligent for a number of reasons. First, it is an admission to yourself that you are not properly prepared. If you have followed the advice throughout this book, you will be very well prepared and you do not need to steal anyone else's argument. Preparation leads to confidence. Confidence in turn results in a better presentation. A better presentation means a greater chance of doing well in the competition.

Second, if you adopt a new argument from someone else's submission, it will be impossible to work through every twist and turn of the argument the night before you are to present it. Even if you study long into the night, there will simply not be enough time. Remember how long you have spent developing your existing arguments. The only certain consequence of spending most of the night before the moot on a new argument is that you will be tired the next day. If you do not thoroughly understand the argument, it will be reflected in your submission. You will not know what questions to expect. You will not necessarily know the relationship it may have to other aspects of your team's submissions. You are likely to pause and hesitate during your presentation because you are still thinking about how to formulate the argument. Your apprehension over this new argument is likely to undermine the persuasiveness of your submission generally.

Thirdly, remember that winning a moot competition is not about winning the case. A well-prepared and polished submission, for whichever side, has a much better chance of scoring well than a more innovative but less well-prepared one.

Almost all competitions allow competitors to view the finals. If you do find yourself watching rather than participating in a final, it is very important to be gracious in defeat. It can be very difficult to watch finals because if you have gone through months of preparation you will always think you could have done better. We touched on a similar point in the section on working in a team, headed "Continue the team work" (pages 92–3). As we have already discussed, sitting in the audience is very different from presenting the case, and while you might think you know how you would respond to a question you can never be sure. Do not devalue someone's achievement just to make yourself feel better. Be happy for those who win, just as you would hope they would be happy for you.

Although it may only provide cold comfort, it is also very beneficial to reflect on how finals are judged, particularly if you have lost a final. Each competition is different; however, what is common to nearly all is that the judging style in the finals will change from the judging style in the general rounds. Those moots that do have a number of general rounds generally ask the moot masters to give a team or an individual a mark. At the end of the general rounds these marks are totalled and the highest-scoring teams proceed to the finals. Because a score is given and a total taken, moot masters in these general rounds can give each student the same score if they wish. They are not actually forced to decide who was better. In essence there does not need to be a loser. However, in final rounds there must be a winner and consequently a loser. As a result, chance plays a much greater part in whether you proceed or leave the competition, which increases the potential for a seemingly "unjust" decision. On many occasions, the audience favourite has not been the winner. Unfortunately, that is just life. Sometimes the luck will run with you, and sometimes it will run against you. How you respond is a measure of the sort of person you are.

## WHAT TO DO WHEN YOU ARE NOT MOOTING

There are two sorts of activities you can do when you are not actually mooting: those that are moot-related and those that are not. Moot-related activities include such things as participating in more practice moots and doing more research. These can be very important but are not much fun. Typically they involve sitting in your hotel room surrounded by the same material that has consumed your life for the past few months while a world of new experiences beckons outside the door. The decision to work or explore should be a hard one. On the one hand you will want to do well in the competition and maybe, just maybe, you will suddenly discover the magic argument that had been eluding you all this time. On the other hand if you leave your hotel room you are guaranteed to learn something new. It will be a difficult decision because you will want to make sure that you have been committed to your task and given your best effort. But if you think about it rationally, that is why you do all those hours of preparation before you arrive.

Everything we have discussed in this book so far, all the time you have spent preparing, brings us to this point. The ultimate secret of success is to have fun! This is a genuine and very serious objective intended to help you reach your greatest potential in the competition. If you enjoy the experience, you will have succeeded in more ways than you will be able to recognise immediately.

It has been emphasised throughout the book how important it is to feel comfortable during your presentation. If you are unhappy about being at the moot, it is guaranteed that you will not feel comfortable. Furthermore, participants who are feeling uncomfortable are unlikely to put in their best effort. They lack the desire and commitment. Put simply, they just do not care about what happens. Contrast this with the participants who are there having fun. For many, it will be one of the greatest experiences of their life. Not only will their confidence and expertise as advocates be growing, they will be meeting new friends, finding out about new cultures and seeing the world.

The opportunities to interact with other participants may be many and varied. Some moots have organised social programs in the evenings, which you should take full advantage of. Even if there is no such program, organise to meet others at a venue somewhere. Spend a bit of time getting to know people. You have one very significant thing in common: your participation in the moot. Other participants will have gone through very similar preparation and will understand issues in a way that many of your existing friends will not. Many participants develop particularly strong and enduring friendships, irrespective of where in the world they happen to live. There may only be one winner of the competition, but if you enjoy your experience you are guaranteed success!

# Chapter 9

# After it's all over

## MAKE THE MOST OF YOUR OPPORTUNITIES

Although it may be desirable that everyone gets the opportunity to participate in an international moot competition, the current reality is that only a very small percentage of students do. This distinguishes participants from the hundreds of thousands of law students around the world who graduate each year. It is very important, therefore, that you do not waste the unique opportunity you have been given.

The wider legal profession plays a role in every international moot competition. Members of the profession may have written the problem, they may be your moot masters, or they might sponsor a prize or event. Importantly for you, they will be at the moot. Although what you know is extremely important, so is who you know, so take this opportunity to have these members of the profession meet you and get to know you. It is not enough for you to simply know who they are from their appearance at the moot; you need to meet them personally so they will remember you.

Your schedule at the competition may be so hectic that there is insufficient time to make the contacts you would like to. That does not mean that you have missed an opportunity. The moot provides you with an introduction to contact someone even after you have returned home. Send that person an email, identify yourself as a participant and begin a dialogue. If you feel reticent about sending an email in this way, find an "official" reason to contact the person. Active involvement in an alumni association is often a very easy way to find official reasons to contact people. If the moot does not have an official alumni association, consider starting one. Naturally you should seek the approval of the competition directors before doing so.

The Moot Alumni Association of the Vis Moot is a very good example. The MAA was started in 1996 by four participants from Cologne, Germany. Initially the MAA was intended to be a way of keeping past participants in contact and to assist with organising the social activities that accompanied the moot. In the past 10 years it has grown into an extremely large and significant contributor to the fields of international commercial law and arbitration. The MAA produces its own internationally renowned law journal. It runs conferences and is even a delegate (without voting power) at UNCITRAL sessions.

Another option that will raise your personal profile in the profession is to convert all that time-consuming and detailed research into a published article. It is not an overstatement to suggest that you will be one of the most knowledgeable people in the world on your topic by the time you compete in the moot. Even if you videotape your performance, the way you used all the information you have gained will only really live on in your memory. Whereas, if you commit your work to paper, that work may one day play a significant role in a real case. Next year it might be your name that appears in the list of references of a team's written document!

## HELP SUBSEQUENT TEAMS

The very last secret of success is to pass on what you have learned. At the beginning of this book, we discussed who could help you as you embarked upon your journey. One of the groups of people referred to were former participants. Former participants are among the best people to help prepare a moot team for competition. Their experience is invaluable. They have actually sat in the same chairs and stood at the same lecterns. These people know the sorts of emotions you will be feeling. They will have undoubtedly made mistakes you can learn from. Who better to help you become comfortable and familiar in the competition setting than someone who has actually been there?

When the competition is all over and you have returned home, take some time to reflect upon your experience. If you have had an enjoyable time make sure you do all that you can to ensure subsequent participants do as well.

Congratulations and good luck!

Part 2

# References and resources

This part of the book contains a list of references relevant to topics covered by international moot competitions. In many instances the annotated references have been provided. The list contains details of books and websites, but not journals or individual articles.

# COMPETITION SPECIFIC/MOOTING SKILLS
## Annotated references
### Websites
www.cambridgemooting.com/2005/

This Cambridge University site provides a short but useful guide to mooting.

www.mootingnet.org.uk/

The Mooting Net site is primarily designed for UK moot participants. However, it does contain advice that is broadly applicable to anyone participating in a moot. There are also a number of links to various other moot related websites.

### Books
#### *Jessup Moot*
C E Schjatvet and Z Hafez, *ILSA Guide to International Moot Court Competition* (2003). International Law Institute, Washington DC

This is an excellent text for anyone participating in the Jessup Moot. The authors are former participants and ILSA is the organisation that runs the moot. The book deals with many competition-specific questions about presentation and style.

#### *Vis Moot*
K P Berger and S G Hoffmann, *Arbitration Interactive: A Case Study for Students and Practitioners* (2002). P Lang, New York

This book–DVD combination provides a very useful introduction to international arbitration. Viewers are taken step by step through a mock arbitration, both on the screen and in the text. The "actors" are all prominent international arbitration practitioners.

## *General*

T Gygar and A Cassimatis, *Moots* (1997). Butterworths, Sydney

Much of this text is devoted to setting up and running a moot program.

J Snape and G Watt, *The Cavendish Guide to Mooting* (2000). Cavendish, London

This was one of the first books published on mooting. It has a strong focus on UK courts.

# LEGAL WRITING AND RESEARCH
## Annotated references
### Websites
www.ualr.edu/cmbarger/

This site describes itself as "[a] website of writing, research, and advocacy resources for law students". The links contained under the Writer's Resources tab are of most use. The article by Professor Ruth Anne Robbins entitled "Painting with Print" is very interesting.

http://law.uvic.ca:8080/legalwriting/index.html

The website of the Legal Writing Centre uses a series of links to provide users with a variety of information and examples of writing.

### Books
A Enquist and L C Oates, *Just Writing: Grammar, Punctuation, and Style for the Legal Writer* (2005). Aspen Publishers, New York

This is a particularly useful text on legal writing. It examines grammar, punctuation, paragraph and sentence construction and effective word choice. It also has a chapter specifically written for those for whom English is a second language.

### Further references
C M Bast and M Hawkins, *Foundations of Legal Research and Writing* (2001). Thomson Learning, Albany, NY

E Campbell and R G Fox, *Students' Guide to Legal Writing and Law Exams* (2003). Federation Press, Leichhardt, NSW

M E McCallum, D A Schmedemann and C L Kunz, *Synthesis: Legal Reading, Reasoning, and Writing in Canada* (2003). CCH Canada, Canada

R K Neumann, *Legal Reasoning and Legal Writing: Structure, Strategy, and Style* (2005). Aspen Publishers, New York

D A Schmedemann and C L Kunz, *Synthesis: Legal Reading, Reasoning, and Writing* (2003). Aspen Law and Business, Gaithersburg

L Webley, *Legal Writing* (2005), Cavendish, London

# INTERNATIONAL COMMERCIAL ARBITRATION
## Annotated references
### Websites
www.lib.uchicago.edu/~llou/intlarb.html

This website was complied by Lyonette Louis-Jacques, foreign and international law librarian and lecturer in law at the D'Angelo Law Library, University of Chicago Law School. It is a fantastic resource, with a considerable number of international commercial arbitration references and links. Unfortunately the site does not appear to have been updated since 15 October 2003.

www.llrx.com/features/arbitration2.htm

This is another website with a multitude of arbitration references and links. It was compiled by Jean M Wenger, the government documents/foreign and international law librarian at the Cook County Law Library. It was last updated on 24 May 2004.

### Books
H C Alvarez, N Kaplan and D Rivkin, eds, *Model Law Decisions: Cases Applying the UNCITRAL Model Law on International Commercial Arbitration [1985–2001]* (2003). Kluwer Law International, New York

This text provides a very useful examination of how the UNCITRAL Model Law on International Commercial Arbitration has been interpreted by common law courts.

R D Bishop, *The Art of Advocacy in International Arbitration* (2004). Juris Publishing, Huntington NY

This book provides a country-by-country analysis of advocacy in international arbitration. Arbitrators from different jurisdictions have different expectations and approaches. It can be very useful to have an appreciation of these before arriving at the competition.

W L Craig, W W Park and J Paulsson, *International Chamber of Commerce Arbitration* (1998). Oceana Publications, Dobbs Ferry NY

Craig, Park and Paulsson is a very oft-cited text on ICC arbitration in particular, and international arbitration generally.

I I Dore, *The UNCITRAL Framework for Arbitration in Contemporary Perspective* (1993). Graham & Trotman/Martinus Nijhoff, Boston, London

UNCITRAL has had a significant influence on international arbitration, and this book provides insights into the field.

P Fouchard, B Goldman, J Savage and E Gaillard, *Fouchard, Gaillard, Goldman on International Commercial Arbitration* (1999). Kluwer Law International, The Hague, Boston

This book is a seminal text in the field of international arbitration. It has a civil law focus.

R Garnett, H Gabriel, J Waincymer and J Epstein, *A Practical Guide to International Commercial Arbitration* (2000). Oceana Publications, New York

This relatively short book is a good entry-level text.

A Redfern and M Hunter, *Law and Practice of International Commercial Arbitration* (2003). Sweet & Maxwell, London

This is another seminal text in the field of international arbitration. It is written from a common law perspective. A student edition is also available, which has the same substantive commentary but does not include the appendixes.

A J van den Berg, *Improving the Efficiency of Arbitration Agreements and Awards: 40 Years of Application of the New York Convention* (1999). Kluwer Law International, The Hague, Boston

Albert van den Berg is one of the world's leading authorities on the enforcement of arbitral awards. Understanding the differences between instruments like the New York Convention and the UNCITRAL Model Law on International Arbitration can often generate innovative arguments.

B Wheeler, *International Arbitration Rules: A Comparative Guide* (2000). LLP, London

Comparative works are always useful. Examining the differences between rules can often be a persuasive technique to explain your argument.

# INTERNATIONAL COURT OF JUSTICE
## Selected references
### Website
www.icj-cij.org/icjwww/icjhome.htm

The official website of the International Court of Justice is user-friendly and contains a considerable amount of information. The Decisions tab not only contains decisions and rulings of the ICJ but often copies of pleadings and submissions.

### Books
P H F Bekker, *World Court Decisions at the Turn of the Millennium (1997–2001)*, (2002). Martinus Nijhoff, The Hague, London

R Hofmann, *World Court Digest* (1993). Springer, Berlin, New York

E McWhinney, *The World Court and the Contemporary International Lawmaking Process* (1979). Alphen aan den Rijn, Sijthoff & Noordhoff, International Publishers

H Meyer, *The World Court In Action: Judging Among the Nations* (2002). Rowman & Littlefield Publishers, Lanham MD

S Muller, D Raic and J M Thuránszky, *The International Court of Justice: Its Future Role After Fifty Years* (1997). Martinus Nijhoff, The Hague, Boston

B N Patel, *The World Court Reference Guide: Judgments, Advisory Opinions and Orders of the Permanent Court of International Justice and the International Court of Justice (1922–2000)* (2002). Kluwer Law International, The Hague, Boston

S Rosenne and T D Gill, *The World Court: What It Is and How It Works* (1989). Kluwer Academic Publishers, Dordrecht, Boston

# INTERNATIONAL COMMERCIAL LAW
## Annotated references
### Websites
www.cisg.law.pace.edu/

This website is arguably the most comprehensive collection of freely available commentary on the CISG. It is an easily navigated site. The annotated guide to the CISG is particularly useful. The site is maintained by Professor Albert Kritzer of Pace University Law School.

### www.llrx.com/features/trade3.htm

The "Revised Guide to International Trade Law Sources on the Internet" by Marci Hoffman provides a very useful introduction to using the internet as a research tool. The site is easy to use and contains many links.

### www.lib.uchicago.edu/~llou/forintlaw.html

"Legal Research on International Law Issues Using the Internet" is an extremely valuable resource for anyone doing general research in international law. There are hundreds of links dealing with a wide variety of international law issues, ranging from international commercial law to humanitarian law.

### ww.asil.org/resource/pil1.htm

ASIL Guide to Electronic Resources for International Law provides numerous links to primary international commercial law documents. It also contains information about other fee-charging services.

### www.wto.org

The WTO website is one of the best international institutional websites. It is easily understood and contains an extraordinary amount of information. The online tutorials and webcasts are particularly informative.

### www.uncitral.org

The UNCITRAL website can be viewed in a number of different languages. Official documents can be easily obtained. The Digests and CLOUT (case law) will often point researchers in the right direction.

### www.unidroit.org/

UNIDROIT is the International Institute for the Unification of Private Law. Various articles from the Uniform Law Review are available free of charge on the website.

## Books

H Bernstein and J M Lookofsky, *Understanding the CISG in Europe* (2003). Kluwer Law International, The Hague, London

Bernstein's text provides a useful discussion of the application of the CISG in Europe. It discusses the practical realities of the CISG rather than just the theoretical aspects.

C M Bianca and M J Bonell, eds, *Commentary on the International Sales Law: The 1980 Vienna Sales Convention* (1987). Giuffrè, Milan

This text provides a comprehensive discussion of each article of the CISG. It is very often referred to in the Vis Moots. It is available online free of charge at the Institute of International Commercial Law at Pace University: www.http://www.cisg.law.pace.edu/

L A DiMatteo, *International Sales Law: An Analysis of CISG Jurisprudence* (2005). Cambridge University Press, Cambridge, New York

This text provides a good introduction to the CISG.

F Ferrari, R A Brand and H Flecher, *The Draft UNCITRAL Digest And Beyond: Cases, Analysis and Unresolved Issues in the UN Sales Convention: Papers of the Pittsburgh Conference Organized by the Center of International Legal Education (CILE)* (2004). Thomson, Sweet & Maxwell, London

The Draft UNCITRAL digest is a particularly useful guide to the CISG case law. UNCITRAL intend to make the digest available on their website when it is completed (www.uncitral.org). The advantage of this text is that it provides commentary.

H D Gabriel, *Practitioner's Guide to the Convention on Contracts for the International Sale of Goods (CISG) and the Uniform Commercial Code (UCC)* (1994). Oceana Publications, New York

Professor Henry Gabriel is the official UCC reporter. The UCC is an American instrument. This text is particularly useful when attempting to distinguish between a UCC interpretation of the CISG and a broader, more internationally based one.

J Honnold, *Uniform Law for International Sales Under the 1980 United Nations Convention* (1999). Kluwer Law International, The Hague

This text by John Honnold was one of the first and most important commentaries on the CISG. It is written from an American (UCC) perspective.

J M Lookofsky, *Understanding the CISG in the USA: A Compact Guide to the 1980 United Nations Convention on Contracts for the International Sale of Goods* (1995). Kluwer Law International, The Hague

This book provides a good summary of American jurisprudence on the CISG up to 1995.

M C Pryles, J Waincymer and M Davies, *International Trade Law: Commentary and Materials* (2004). Lawbook Company, Pyrmont NSW

This is a cases and commentary text on international commercial law generally. It provides useful explanations of the CISG, Incoterms and WTO.

P Schlechtriem and I Schwenzer, eds, *Commentary on the UN Convention on the International Sale of Goods (CISG)* (2005). Oxford University Press, Oxford

This is a seminal CISG text. It is possibly the most cited text on the subject. The book is quite easy to read and provides a very useful introduction to the topic.

*United Nations Conference on Contracts for the International Sale of Goods, Vienna, 10 March–11 April 1980: Official Records: Documents of the Conference and Summary Records of the Plenary Meetings and the Meetings of the Main Committees* (1981). United Nations, New York

When examining any international instrument it is always advisable to obtain any preliminary or preparatory documents used by the drafters. Examining the alterations and editions made by them provides considerable insight into the intended meaning. The travaux préparatoire for the CISG is available online free of charge at the Institute of International Commercial Law at Pace University: www.http://www.cisg.law.pace.edu/

M R Will, *Twenty Years of International Sales Law Under the CISG: The UN Convention on Contracts for the International Sale of Goods: International Bibliography and Case Law Digest, 1980–2000* (2000). Kluwer Law International, The Hague, Boston

This is a good summary of CISG case law.

B Zeller, *Damages under the Convention on Contracts for the International Sale of Goods* (2005). Oceana Publications, Dobbs Ferry NY

As the title suggests, this book focuses specifically on the issue of damages in the CISG. It provides a useful comparison between the treatment of damages in a number of international instruments.

# INTELLECTUAL PROPERTY
# Annotated references
## Websites
www.llrx.com/features/iplaw.htm

This site by Stephanie Weigmann provides a good introduction to researching intellectual property issues. It sets out various areas of research and provides links to many of the documents and institutions discussed.

www.oiprc.ox.ac.uk/links.html

This site offers very comprehensive coverage of useful links for intellectual property law.

www.wipo.int

This is the official site for the World Intellectual Property Organisation. It contains general material on intellectual property law, e-books on intellectual property law, and international documents, including draft documents, on intellectual property law.

www.wto.org

This is the official site for the World Trade Organisation. It contains material on trade-related aspects of intellectual property rights.

www.patent.gov.uk/

This is a user-friendly site with useful basic information.

## Books
L Bently and B Sherman, *Intellectual Property Law* (2004). Oxford University Press, New York

This book provides a very detailed account of the law. It is a helpful starting point for those who have specific research ideas.

W A Copinger, E P Skone James, K M Garnett, G Davies and G Harbottle, *Copinger and Skone James on Copyright* (2005). Sweet & Maxwell, London

This is a classic volume on copyright. The coverage is comprehensive of the subject and concise on each point. With its longevity, tracing earlier editions gives a historical perspective.

W R Cornish and D Llewelyn, *Intellectual Property: Patents, Copyright, Trade Marks, and Allied Rights* (2003). Sweet & Maxwell, London

This book provides a comprehensive and critical approach to the law. The detailed footnotes are very useful.

T Hart and L Fazzani, *Intellectual Property Law* (2004). Palgrave Macmillan, Basingstoke

This book gives a very brief and general overview of the law. The fourth edition will be published in 2007.

D M Kerly and D Kitchin, *Kerly's Law of Trade Marks and Trade Names* (2005). Sweet & Maxwell, London

This classic volume on trade marks gives a comprehensive coverage of the subject and is concise on each point. With its longevity tracing earlier editions gives a historical perspective.

J McCarthy, *The Rights of Publicity and Privacy* (2000). C Boardman, New York

This looseleaf service provides a good coverage with a useful and detailed table of contents.

M B Nimmer and D Nimmer, *Nimmer on Copyright: A Treatise on the Law of Literary, Musical and Artistic Property, and the Protection of Ideas* (1997). M Bender, New York

This looseleaf service provides a good coverage and a useful and detailed table of contents.

S Thorley, R Miller, G Burkill and C Birss, *Terrell on the Law of Patents* (2006). Sweet & Maxwell, London

This classic volume on patents offers a comprehensive coverage of the subject and is concise on each point.

## Further references

J Drexl and A Kur, *Intellectual Property and Private International Law: Heading for the Future* (2005). Hart Publishing, Oxford, Portland OR
C E F Rickett and G W Austin, *International Intellectual Property and the Common Law World* (2000). Hart Publishing, Oxford

# INTERNATIONAL LAW (GENERAL)
# Selected references

### Website
http://www.mpil.de/ww/en/pub/news.cfm

Using the Max Planck Institute website, it is possible to search the institute's library catalogue and thereby uncover possible resources. Some full-text publications are also freely available on the site, such as the *World Court Digest*. To find these publications use the "quickfind" function in the top right corner, select "publications", and then publications by the Institute.

### Books
A Aust, *Modern Treaty Law and Practice* (2000). Cambridge University Press, New York

R Bernhardt, *Encyclopedia of Public International Law, Vol. 1 (US)* (1981). North-Holland Publishing Company, Amsterdam, New York

J L Brierly and H Waldock, *The Law of Nations: An Introduction to the International Law of Peace* (1963). Oxford University Press, Oxford

I Brownlie, *The Rule of Law In International Affairs: International Law at the Fiftieth Anniversary of the United Nations* (1998). Martinus Nijhoff Publishers, Kluwer Law International, The Hague, Boston

I Brownlie, *Basic Documents in International Law* (2002). Oxford University Press, Oxford, New York

I Brownlie, *Principles of Public International Law* (2003). Oxford University Press, Oxford

A Cassese, *International Law* (2005). Oxford University Press, Oxford

T M Franck, *Fairness in International Law and Institutions* (1995). Oxford University Press, Oxford

P Malanczuk and M Akehurst, *Akehurst's Modern Introduction to International Law* (1997). Routledge, London, New York

S Rosenne, *Practice and Methods of International Law* (1984). Oceana Publications, London, New York

S Rosenne, *The International Law Commission's Draft Articles on State Responsibility: Part 1, Articles 1–35* (1991). Kluwer Academic Publishers, Boston

S Rosenne, *The Perplexities of Modern International Law* (2004). Martinus Nijhoff, Leiden, Boston

D Sarooshi, *International Organizations and their Exercise of Sovereign Powers* (2005). Oxford University Press, Oxford, New York

O Schachter, *International Law in Theory and Practice* (1991). Kluwer Academic Publishers, Dordrecht, Boston

O Schachter and M Ragazzi, *International Responsibility Today: Essays in Memory of Oscar Schachter* (2005). Brill, Leiden, Boston

M N Shaw, *International Law* (2003). Cambridge University Press, New York

B Simma, *The Charter of the United Nations: A Commentary* (2002). Oxford University Press, Oxford

J H W Verzijl, W P Heere and J P S Offerhaus, *International Law in Historical Perspective* (1968). A W Sijthoff, Leyden

K Wellens, *Resolutions and Statements of the United Nations Security Council (1946–2000): A Thematic Guide* (2001). Kluwer Law International, The Hague, Boston

# HUMANITARIAN LAW/ARMED INTERVENTION
## Selected references
### Books

F K Abiew, *The Evolution of the Doctrine and Practice of Humanitarian Intervention* (1999). Kluwer Law International, The Hague, London

A C Arend and R J Beck, *International Law and the Use of Force: Beyond the UN Charter Paradigm* (1993). Routledge, London, New York

I Brownlie, *International Law and the Use of Force by States* (1981). Oxford University Press, Oxford

I Brownlie and F M Brookfield, *Treaties and Indigenous Peoples* (1992). Clarendon Press, Oxford

S Carlson and G Gisvold, *Practical Guide to the International Covenant on Civil and Political Rights (ICCPR)* (2003). Transnational Publishers, Ardsley NY

P A Fernandez-Sanchez, *New Challenges of Humanitarian Law in Armed Conflict* (2005). Martinus Nijhoff, Leiden

D Fleck and S Addy, *The Handbook of the Law of Visiting Forces* (2001). Oxford University Press, Oxford

D Fleck and M Bothe, *The Handbook of Humanitarian Law in Armed Conflicts* (1995). Oxford University Press, New York

T M Franck, *Recourse to Force: State Action Against Threats and Armed Attacks* (2002). Cambridge University Press, New York

C Gray, *International Law and the Use of Force* (2004). Oxford University Press, London

L C Green, *The Contemporary Law of Armed Conflict* (2000). Manchester University Press, Manchester

L Henkin *The International Bill of Rights: The Covenant on Civil and Political Rights* (1981). Columbia University Press, New York

S Joseph, M Castan and J Schultz, *The International Covenant on Civil and Political Rights: Cases, Materials, and Commentary* (2004). Oxford University Press, Oxford

R O Keohane and J L Holzgrefe, *Humanitarian Intervention: Ethical, Legal and Political Dilemmas* (2003). Cambridge University Press, Cambridge

G Kewley, *Humanitarian Law in Armed Conflicts* (1993). Australian Red Cross, East Melbourne

R B Lillich, *The Human Rights of Aliens in Contemporary International Law* (1984). Manchester University Press, Manchester, Dover NH

N S Rodley, *The Treatment of Prisoners under International Law* (1987). UNESCO, Oxford University Press, Paris, New York

N S Rodley, *To Loose the Bands of Wickedness: International Intervention In Defence of Human Rights* (1992). Macmillan, New York

J M Welsh, *Humanitarian Intervention and International Relations* (2004). Oxford University Press, Oxford, New York

# ENVIRONMENTAL LAW

## Selected references

### Books

P M Haas, R O Keohane and M A Levy, *Institutions for the Earth: Sources of Effective International Environmental Protection* (1993). MIT Press, Cambridge MA

R O Keohane and M A Levy, *Institutions for Environmental Aid: Pitfalls and Promise* (1996). MIT Press, Cambridge MA

B Rüster, B Simma, A Schmidt and G Marx-Zimmerer, *International Protection of the Environment: Treaties and Related Documents* (1990). Oceana Publications, Dobbs Ferry NY

N Schrijver, *Sovereignty Over Natural Resources: Balancing Rights and Duties* (1997). Cambridge University Press, Cambridge, New York

# MARITIME LAW
## Selected references
### Websites
www.admiraltylawguide.com/

The Admiralty and Maritime Law Guide purports to have "over 1,500 annotated links to Admiralty law resources on the internet and a growing database of Admiralty case digests, opinions and international maritime conventions".

www.ll.georgetown.edu/find/resource_display_subject. cfm?topic_id=166

This website provides a brief but annotated list of maritime resources, both hard-copy texts and internet resources. It has a US focus.

www.imo.org

This is the official website of the International Marine Organisation.

### Books
R P Anand, *Origin and Development of the Law of the Sea: History of International Law Revisited* (1983). Martinus Nijhoff, Kluwer, The Hague, Boston

R R Churchill and A V Lowe, *The Law of the Sea* (1999). Manchester University Press, Manchester

H Karan, *The Carrier's Liability under International Maritime Conventions: The Hague, Hague-Visby, and Hamburg Rules* (2005). E. Mellen Press, Lewiston NY

S Marr, *The Precautionary Principle in the Law of the Sea: Modern Decision Making in International Law* (2003). Martinus Nijhoff, The Hague

K Michel, *War, Terror and Carriage by Sea* (2004). LLP, London

D P O'Connell and I A Shearer, *The International Law of the Sea* (1982). Clarendon Press, Oxford, New York

R. Platzöder, *The Law of The Sea: Documents, 1983–1989: Preparatory Commission for the International Sea-Bed Authority and for the International Tribunal* (1990). Oceana Publications, Dobbs Ferry NY

F D Rose, *Maritime Law* (1988). Sweet & Maxwell, Carswell, London; Agincourt, Ontario

B J Theutenberg, *The Evolution of the Law of the Sea: A Study of Resources and Strategy with Special Regard to the Polar Regions* (1984). Tycooly International Publications, Dublin

D Walsh, *The Law of the Sea: Issues in Ocean Resource Management* (1977). Praeger, New York

# Part 3

# International moots

# WILLEM C VIS INTERNATIONAL COMMERCIAL ARBITRATION MOOT

The following information has been reprinted from the competition website with permission.

## Contact

Professor Eric E Bergsten
Schimmelgasse 16/16
A-1030 Vienna, Austria

Phone and fax: +43 1 713-5408
E-mail: eric.bergsten@chello.at
Website: http://www.cisg.law.pace.edu/vis.html

## When

The Problem is distributed on the first Friday in October. It is distributed by posting on the Moot website. A memorandum supporting the position of the claimant is due in Vienna early in December. Each participating team is sent a copy of the memorandum for claimant of one of the other teams in the Moot. A memorandum for respondent is prepared in response to the memorandum received, and is due in Vienna in mid-February. The oral arguments take place in Vienna, beginning on the Saturday a week prior to Easter and closing on Thursday of Easter week. The general rounds of the oral arguments take place at the Law Faculty of the University of Vienna (Juridicum) on Saturday through Tuesday. Elimination rounds among the highest-ranking teams take place on Wednesday and Thursday, culminating in the final argument. The Moot closes with an awards banquet following the final argument.

## Where

The oral hearings will be held primarily at the Faculty of Law (Juridicum) of the University of Vienna, Schottenbastei 10-16, A-1010 Vienna, with additional hearings at the offices of the law firm Dorda Brugger Jordis, Dr Karl Lueger, Ring 10, A-1010 Vienna.

## Subject matter

The Moot involves a dispute arising out of a contract of sale between two countries that are party to the United Nations Convention on Contracts for the International Sale of Goods. The contract provides that any dispute that might arise is to be settled by arbitration in Danubia, a country that has enacted the UNCITRAL Model Law on International Commercial Arbitration and is a party to the Convention on the Recognition and Enforcement of Foreign Arbitral Awards. The arbitral rules to be applied rotate yearly among the arbitration rules of co-sponsors of the Moot.

## Structure of the moot

The business community's marked preference for resolving international commercial disputes by arbitration is the reason this method of dispute resolution was selected as the clinical tool to train law students through two crucial phases: the writing of memorandums for claimant and respondent and the hearing of oral argument based upon the memorandums – both settled by arbitral experts in the issues considered. The forensic and written exercises require determining questions of contract, flowing from a transaction relating to the sale or purchase of goods under the United Nations Convention on Contracts for the International Sale of Goods and other uniform international commercial law, in the context of an arbitration of a dispute under specified arbitration rules.

In the pairings of teams for each general round of the forensic and written exercises, every effort is made to have civil law schools argue against common law schools, so that each may learn from approaches taken by persons trained in another legal culture. Similarly, the teams of arbitrators judging each round are from both common law and civil law backgrounds.

Each team will argue four times in the general rounds, twice as claimant and twice as respondent. In its first two oral hearings, each team will argue once as claimant and once as respondent. The respondent will be the team that prepared the memorandum for respondent in opposition to the memorandum for claimant that was sent to it. In its third and fourth oral hearings the teams will argue against teams with which they were not paired for the purpose of preparing written memoranda.

After the general rounds, the scores of each team for its oral presentation in the four arguments will be totalled. The 32 teams that have obtained the highest composite scores will meet the following Wednesday morning.

## Awards

- Pieter Sanders Award for Best Written Memorandum for Claimant.
- Werner Melis Award for Best Written Memorandum for Respondent.
- Martin Domke Award for Best Individual Oralist. This award for the general rounds will be won by the individual advocate with the highest average score during these rounds. To be eligible for this award a participant must have argued at least once for the claimant and once for the respondent.
- Frédéric Eisemann Award for Best Team Orals. This award will be made to the winning team in the final round of the oral hearings.

## Officially recognised alumni associations

The MAA is the alumni association of the Willem C Vis International Commercial Arbitration Moot. It is an international, decentralised, non-political and non-profit institution serving a network of future leaders in law and business as well as professionals outside the association.

The MAA focuses on the promotion of education in contemporary issues of international commercial law and alternative dispute resolution. The MAA network spans across 33 countries in all continents. The members are professors and research scholars, lawyers and judges, domestic and international civil servants, managers and consultants, as well as young professionals and students striving for a career in such areas.

### Contact

MAA
GPO Box 2216
Melbourne VIC 3001
Australia

Phone: +1 917 640 6120
Fax: +49 40 740 200 2079
Website: http://www.maa.net/

# WILLEM C VIS INTERNATIONAL COMMERCIAL ARBITRATION MOOT (EAST)

## General information

The Vis Moot (East) is a sister moot to the Willem C Vis International Commercial Arbitration Moot, which takes place in Hong Kong. The Vis Moot (East) uses the same Problem and the rules are essentially the same as the Moot that takes place in Vienna. Nevertheless, they are two separate moots with separate registration, including registration fee, and separate winners. The Hong Kong Moot is not a regional elimination moot for the Vienna Moot. A law school can register for the Hong Kong Moot, the Vienna Moot or both. While the same students can be on both teams, a given student cannot argue in both the Hong Kong and the Vienna Moot in the same year.

The following information was provided in part by Ms Louise Barrington. Additional information was reprinted from the competition website with permission.

**Contact**

Louise Barrington
Hong Kong Director
Vis East International Arbitration Moot

Email: louiseb@netvigator.com
Website: http://www.cismoot.org

# When

As is the case for the Willem C Vis International Commercial arbitration moot in Vienna (the Vienna Moot), the problem is distributed on the first Friday in October. A memorandum supporting the position of the claimant is due early in December. Each participating team is sent a copy of the memorandum for claimant of one of the other teams in the Moot. A memorandum for respondent is prepared in response to the memorandum received, and is due in mid-February. The oral arguments take place in Hong Kong about two weeks before or after the Vienna orals.

# Where

The Moot takes place in Hong Kong, the former British colony "repatriated" to China in 1997. It retains its British common law heritage through the "one country, two systems" principle of the basic law. There are three law schools in Hong Kong and the languages spoken are English and Cantonese.

# Subject matter

The Moot involves a dispute arising out of a contract of sale between two countries. At least one country is a party to the United Nations Convention on Contracts for the International Sale of Goods. The contract provides that any dispute that might arise is to be settled by arbitration in Danubia, a country that has enacted the UNCITRAL Model Law on International Commercial Arbitration and is a party to the Convention on the Recognition and Enforcement of Foreign Arbitral Awards. The arbitral rules to be applied change from year to year.

## Structure of the moot

There are no regional rounds. Every team participates in four days of general rounds. The top eight teams proceed to the quarter finals.

## Awards

- Eric Bergsten Award for Best Written Memorandum for Claimant.
- Fali Nariman Award for Best Written Memorandum for Respondent.
- Neil Kaplan Award for Best Individual Oralist. This award for the general rounds will be won by the individual advocate with the highest average score during these rounds. To be eligible for this award a participant must have argued at least once for the claimant and once for the respondent.
- David Hunter Award for Best Team Orals. This award will be made to the winning team in the final round of the oral hearings.

## Officially recognised alumni associations

Moot Alumni Association (same as Vienna Vis Moot)

MAA
GPO Box 2216
Melbourne VIC 3001
Australia

Phone: +1 917 640 6120
Fax: +49 40 74 0200 2079
Website: http://www.maa.net

# PHILIP C JESSUP INTERNATIONAL LAW MOOT COURT COMPETITION

The following information was provided in part by Mr Michael Peil, and obtained from the competition website.

## Contact

International Law Students Association
25 East Jackson Boulevard, Suite 518
Chicago, IL 60604 USA

Phone +1 312 362 5025
Email: ilsa@ilsa.org
Website: http://www.ilsa.org/

# When

The Problem is usually released in September. The applicant and respondent memorials are due around mid January. The regional rounds are held some time in January and February. The international rounds are held in March. Prospective participants should consult the official Moot website for a current schedule.

# Where

The Shearman and Sterling international rounds are held in early April in Washington DC (USA). The international rounds are held in conjunction with, and at the same time and location as, ILSA's Spring Conference and with the annual meeting of the American Society of International Law (ASIL). Participants will therefore have an opportunity to attend a premier international law event during their stay in Washington DC.

The international rounds are a week-long event. In addition to the Competition, there are a number of evening and afternoon social events, designed to introduce the participants to their colleagues (students and practitioners) from around the world. There are almost 90 countries participating and over 1,000 students and practitioners attending the week's events.

# Subject matter

The Jessup Competition is a simulation of oral and written practice before the International Court of Justice. Written and edited over the course of a year by top practitioners and academics, each year's Problem features a hypothetical dispute between two fictional countries, arising under international law. Recent Problems have touched upon international criminal law, international law and the internet, law of the sea, human trafficking, and the law of multinational enterprises.

## Structure of the moot

In addition to the international rounds, the Jessup conducts about 60 regional and national rounds in participant countries around the world. The winners of these regional and national rounds (as well as any solo teams from other countries) advance to the international rounds. National and regional rounds are typically conducted in January and February.

# ANNUAL INTERNATIONAL INTER-UNIVERSITY INTELLECTUAL PROPERTY MOOT AT OXFORD

This Moot is organised by the Oxford Intellectual Property Research Centre (OIPRC) and the Intellectual Property Institute (IPI), London.

The following information was provided by Ms Gillian Brook.

### Contact

Karen Clayton
IP Moot Administrator
OIPRC, St Peter's College
Oxford OX1 2DL, UK.

Phone: +44 018 6527 8952
Fax: +44 018 6527 8959
E-mail: Karen.Clayton@law.ox.ac.uk
Website: http://www.oiprc.ox.ac.uk

## When

The facts and rules are released in December. The deadlines for receipt of two written submissions are in February. The oral weekend is held some time during March/April (during Oxford

University Easter vacation, but not Easter weekend itself). University sities are invited to participate during September and October, and must make two written submissions (one for appellant and one for respondent), which are judged anonymously before being considered for the oral phase. The registration for the oral phase closes a month before the event weekend.

## Where

The oral phase is residential and takes place at an Oxford College over a full weekend. See www.ox.ac.uk for information on the University of Oxford, its Colleges and information for visitors.

## Subject matter

The area of law is intellectual property (IP). The goal of the event is to bring together students and specialist IP practitioners and to encourage research and interest in IP and mooting in universities worldwide. Mooters are encouraged to argue an appeal on principle before the Supreme Court of Erewhon, so that competitors from common law and civilian traditions are placed on an equal footing.

## Structure of the moot

Two written submissions must be submitted in advance of the oral phase. The maximum number of teams in the oral phase is 32. The decision on numbers to be admitted is taken after the written submissions have been made. All teams admitted to the oral phase participate in two rounds, one as the appellant and one as the respondent. The best eight on points go through to round 3, from which point onwards, the competition is knock-out.

Judges up to the final rounds comprise panels of practitioners experienced in intellectual property matters (barristers, solicitors, patent or trade mark attorneys, UK Patent Office hearing officers). The final round is judged by a panel of three IP specialist judges from the English Court of Appeal or High Court. A typical bench has comprised Lords Justices Mummery and Jacob, and Mr Justice Pumfrey of the Patents Court. The judges give short reasons for their judgment based on the arguments presented, before announcing the winning team.

## Cash, book and book voucher prizes

- Winners and runners-up at the Oral Phase Final.
- Best oralist at Oral Phase Rounds 1 and 2.
- Best written submissions.
- Special prizes.

## General information

The inaugural event was in 2003. There is growing worldwide interest as the IP Moot at Oxford sells itself by word of mouth and by those looking for IP events on the web. The event is generously supported by sponsors, which include the IPI, The IP Lawyers Organisation (TIPLO), about 20 legal firms and four publishers. These sponsors provide cash donations, which fund the weekend venue, the prizes, and the meals and accommodation for the mooters, as well as generous gifts of books and journal subscriptions. Mooters pay a token contribution (£20 for the 2006 event).

The spirit of this Moot is "inclusive", and any eligible university that expresses an interest is normally invited. Undergraduate and postgraduate students who have never practised law may compete (see rules for further details on eligibility). There is therefore a wide range of mooters, ranging from those who may have studied law for only one term through to those following a taught postgraduate degree with specialist options in IP.

## 2005 sponsors

### Organisations

Intellectual Property Institute (IPI)
The Intellectual Property Lawyers' Organisation (TIPLO)
Oriel College

### Law firms and chambers

Slaughter and May
Frank B Dehn & Company

Howrey Simon Arnold & White
Simmons & Simmons
Chambers at 8 New Square, Lincoln's Inn
Page White & Farrer
Freshfields Bruckhaus Deringer
J A Kemp & Co
McDermott Will & Emery
Willoughby & Partners
Manches LLP
Bird & Bird
Carpmaels & Ransford
Marks & Clerk
Mewburn Ellis
New Square Chambers, Lincoln's Inn
Morgan Cole
Stikeman Elliott LLP

## Suppliers of prizes
Cambridge University Press
Hart Publishing
Hogarth Chambers
Oxford University Press
Thomson Sweet & Maxwell

## INTERNATIONAL MARITIME MOOT
The following information was provided by Dr Sarah Derrington.

### Contact
Dr Sarah Derrington
T C Beirne School of Law
University of Queensland 4072

Email: s.derrington@law.uq.edu.au
Website: http://www.law.murdoch.edu.au/maritimemoot/
moots.html

## When

Registration is usually held mid-January and the Problem released late January. The claimant memorandum is due in late March and the respondent memorandum is due in early June. The oral rounds are held in late June/early July.

## Where

The location rotates around the region in such locations as Brisbane, Sydney, Perth, Hong Kong and Singapore.

## Subject matter

The Moot is the arbitration of a dispute involving the international carriage of goods by sea.

## Structure of the moot

Each team argues four times in the general rounds, twice for the claimant and twice for the respondent. Quarter-final rounds are held for the top eight teams and semi-final rounds for the top four teams. Two teams go through to the final.

## Awards

- Best Memorandum for the Claimant
- Best Memorandum for the Respondent
- Highest Ranked Team in the General Rounds
- Best Speaker in the General Rounds
- Runner-up Team
- Winning Team
- Best Speaker in the Finals
- Achievement Award

## General information

In 2006, the organisation for the Competition was taken over by Murdoch University in Perth. The academics responsible are Professor Gabriel Moens and Ms Kate Lewins. The moot site has been relocated from the University of Queensland to Murdoch

University, but a link will remain on the University of Queensland website.

# THE TELDERS INTERNATIONAL LAW MOOT COURT COMPETITION

The following information has been obtained from the competition website.

## Contact

Leiden University/Campus The Hague
Lange Houtstraat 7
2511 CV DEN HAAG

Phone: +31 70 302 1070
Fax: +31 70 302 1025

Email: telders@campusdenhaag.nl
Website: http://www.telders.org

## When

The Problem is usually released in September and applications submitted in November. The applicant and respondent memorials due around mid January. The national oral rounds are held in February and the finals late March.

## Where

The finals are conducted in the International Court of Justice, Peace Palace, The Hague, Netherlands.

## Subject matter

The subject of the Moot is a fictitious dispute between two States before the International Court of Justice. Each team comprises four students, and for each European country only the university winning the national rounds may participate in the international rounds held in The Hague. The judges are drawn from the real

International Court of Justice and the Iran–United States Claims Tribunal, and other experts in international law.

## Structure of the moot

Only one university from each country can participate. If multiple universities from one country register, national pre-selection rounds are conducted.

Scores in both the oral and written components of the competition are added together to determine the finalists

## Awards

- The Telders Cup for the team who wins the finals.
- The Max Huber Award for the highest overall score.
- Award for the Best Oralist and Runner-up.
- Awards for the highest team scores for the memorials and for the pleadings.

## JEAN PICTET COMPETITION

The following information has been reprinted from the Competition website with permission.

### Contact

Concours Jean-Pictet
25 rue des Garnaudes\F-63400 Chamalières
Fax: +33 4 7417 7755

Email: info@concourspictet.org
Website: http://www.concourspictet.org

## When

The Problem is usually released in September and applications submitted in November. The Competition takes place in March.

## Where

Every year the Competition takes place in a different location.

# Subject matter

The Jean-Pictet Competition is a week-long training event on international humanitarian law (IHL) intended for students (undergraduate or above in law, political science, military academies, etc). It consists in "taking law out of books", by simulations and role plays, allowing the jury of the Competition to evaluate teams' theoretical knowledge and practical understanding of IHL.

# Structure of the moot

The situations are founded on fictitious, but realistic, scenarios of armed conflict. During the competition, the group dynamics alternate: meetings between the jury and one team, the jury and several teams, and between two teams. Participants and the jury have roles that change – for example, Red Cross delegates in the morning and combatants in the afternoon – encouraging the participants to consider the same situation from a variety of perspectives.

Teams can take part in either the Francophone or the Anglophone session. At the end of each session, the finalists compete in the international final, and the Jean-Pictet Prize is awarded to the best team.

Each team is accompanied throughout the Competition (before, during and after) by a tutor; they receive learning materials regularly to assist with preparation and to improve their command of IHL (as well as human rights law and refugee law). All tests during the Competition are conducted orally – no written submissions are required, other than for the application file.

# General information

Taking part in the competition is a unique experience. Training on the concrete application of IHL is facilitated by the presence of experts (the jury and tutors). Participation also has considerable effect on personal development: through experience of team work, presentation techniques, communication and stress management, as well as offering the opportunity to meeting students coming from the five continents to compete in a friendly tournament on extremely sensitive topics.

For students wishing to work in the fields of IHL, international solidarity, international criminal law and refugee law, participation in the Competition constitutes an important asset in a curriculum vitae.

# ELSA MOOT COURT COMPETITION EMC2

## Contact

International Organising Committee
Fax: +32 2 646 2923

Email: emcc@listserv.elsa.org
Website: http://www.elsa.org/emcc/index.asp

## When

The Problem is usually released in September, and the applicant and respondent memorials are due early January. The regional oral rounds are held in mid March and the finals in late April.

## Where

The finals are conducted in Geneva, Switzerland.

## Subject matter

The Moot involves a dispute between two members of the World Trade Organisation.

## Structure of the moot

Prospective participants should consult the ELSA website as structure varies depending on the country.

# MANFRED LACHS SPACE LAW MOOT COURT COMPETITION

## Contact

Varies depending on location (see website).

Website: http://www.spacemoot.org/

# When

Applications are usually submitted in early January and the applicant and respondent memorials are due around late February. The regional rounds are held in April and the finals in October.

# Where

The location of the finals changes annually.

# Subject matter

The Moot is a space law dispute before the International Court of Justice.

# Structure of the moot

There are two or three students per team. The semi-finals and finals are judged on a combination of oral presentation and memorials.

# Index